MORE THAN RESTORED!

TURNING YOUR MESS INTO YOUR MESSAGE!

DR. JERRY A. GRILLO, JR.

FZM Publishing

Copyright 2012
By God Strong Ministries
P.O. Box 3707 Hickory, NC   28603

All Scriptures, unless indicated, are taken from the King James Version.

Scriptures quotations marked NJKV are taken from the New King James Version.

Scriptures quotations marked NIV are taken from the New International Version.

Scriptures quotations marked NLT are taken from the New Living Translation ®, copyright © 1996, 2004 by Tyndale Charitable Trust. Used by permission of Tyndale House Publishers. All rights reserved.

ISBN
978-0-578-11277-0

Printed in the United States of America.

TABLE OF CONTENT

INTRODUCTION

The Kingdom of God has never been normal. It has never been business as usual. The whole Bible is full of unusual events and testimonies. We must understand that God isn't a God of the usual. He is a God that is unusual. We have to stretch our thinking out of the box of the usual if we are going to understand God's primary purpose.

You must shift your mind for increase and restoration to understand the divine purpose of the Kingdom of God.

RESTORATION IS GETTING BACK AND MORE!

In the natural, restoration means getting back what you've lost. In the Kingdom, restoration is more than God fixing what has been broken or replacing what was lost. It is God's intention to restore and put more back. Restoration carries with it a powerful law. It is the law of increase.

Let me explain. If you bought a 1967 Chevy in 1967, it would cost you around two thousand dollars. If you take that same car out of a junkyard and restore it to its original condition, the 1967 Chevy that once only cost two thousand dollars is now worth over forty thousand.

The old car, that at one time was once new, became used and abused. It was taken to the junk yard after it couldn't go any further and thrown in a pile to be forgotten about. Over time the seats ripped, the dashboard cracked and faded and the tires dry rotted. The outside became rusted and the engine clogged up. However, someone came along and could see the value in the car even if it was wasted and in a useless state. This is exactly what God does for us! The Holy Spirit notices our pile of rejection, pain and failure, and just like that car, God can and will pull us out of our pit and "work on" us and restore what seasons of loss have stolen.

Restoration has quite a few meanings.

1. **Restore**
2. **Repair**
3. **Rebuild**
4. **Rekindle**
5. **Reconnect**
6. **Realign**
7. **Readjust**
8. **Recommit**
9. **Reorganize**
10. **Remove**
11. **Rearrange**

We have to understand what the thing we are restoring looked like in its original state. We have to have knowledge of the architect that designed it. Once that is complete, someone has to put all the pieces together and make sure they are in working order. Then, and only then, will something be fully restored. Then the thing that was useless becomes useful again and worth more than it was at its inception.

*"As I watched, this horn **was waging war** against the holy people **and defeating them**, until the Ancient of Days came and pronounced judgment in favor of the holy people of the Most High, and the time came when they possessed the kingdom."*
Daniel 7:21- 22

Notice the horn, which is the enemy, is waging war against the people of the Most High and prevailing!
There will always be a time when the enemy appears to be advancing and winning over your lives. In those seasons, you feel like all hell has been let loose. You are pushed, pulled, rejected, hurt, lied to, beat on and left for lost.
Things aren't always as they appear. Don't get me wrong; the enemy is prevailing during this season. Your mind, body, soul and spirit are taking the hit. Your marriage, your finances and

everything you hold dear are stolen and lost in this time of attack. I know at this moment in your life it feels like it is never going to let up!

You must understand that the enemy appears to be winning in this season. The horn was prevailing, but that's not where the story ended. This is not where it is going to end with you either. Your season will change! This reminds me of a story I once heard.

A father had four sons. When they were young men, he wanted to teach them not to make quick and harsh judgments on people and in life's circumstances.

So he sent them on a quest, a journey to visit a pear tree that was a long way off. He sent the first son (oldest) in winter, the second in spring, the third in summer and the youngest in fall.

When they all returned, the father sat them down and asked them to report what they had seen and learned about the pear tree. The first son, the oldest, said, "Well, what I witnessed was a dead, dried up and twisted tree". The second son said, "I disagree. When I saw the pear tree it was budding and had signs of life and potential all over it." The third son replied,

Don't Allow the Voice of Comfort to Speak Louder Than the Voice of Purpose!

"Oh, you're mistaken. When I arrived the tree was full of blooming flowers that had the sweetest fragrance and full of leaves." The youngest said, "You are all wrong. When I saw the tree it was full of the sweetest and plumpest fruit. The tree was huge and in full array."

The four sons looked at their father puzzled. "How can this be?" they enquired. The father said,"Sons, you are all right. What you have to understand is that each of you only saw the tree in one season of its life. When you are living life and looking at others, remember you are only witnessing one season. Don't throw in the towel or judge someone too quickly. You may be in your winter season and everything around you looks dried up, dead and useless. All you are witnessing is the preparation of spring's renewal and summer's flowers and fall's harvests. Learn to wait for all four seasons before you make a call or judgment. [i]

This is exactly what happened in Daniel chapter seven. For a season, the Horn, *the enemy* was prevailing. That was only winter and it was before the Ancient of Days appeared.

Ancient of Days or Ancient One, is actually the root meaning for the word Architect. The word Architect comes from the word Archaic. The Ancient One, or Ancient of Days, is actually a type and shadow of Jesus. Look at it again. *"The horn, enemy made war against the saints and was winning. Until the Ancient of Days, the ARCHITECT showed up..."* When Jesus the Ancient of Days (the Architect) showed up, He realized that this was not how He had planned things to happen. The Architect looked at the original plans and realized that things were out of order!

There was chaos in the life of the saints. The Architect put it back to its original status and plans. He gave the saints power and favor. This power and favor produces RESTORATION for the saints! God's plan has always been to restore, rebuild, rekindle and reconnect us to His purpose.

RESTORATION REQUIRES CHANGE

Restoration isn't easy. Sometimes when you find yourself restoring something, you realize it may have been easier to buy it new. It takes a different mindset to restore, than to just erase and start over. Restoration is a process. You must understand that just because you decide to be restored doesn't mean that you will get back everything overnight. You must allow time for change and new decisions to take effect.

You must silence all wrong voices around you when you are changing and decide to walk in restoration. Don't allow the voice of comfort to speak louder than the voice of change and purpose!

Spiritual Steps for Restoration:

1. Remove what the years have accumulated.
2. Cleanse yourself from depression, un-forgiveness and bitterness.
3. Saturate your mind with the Word of God.
4. Apply what you have read and heard!
5. Fill your spirit with the Holy Spirit.
6. Cover the old areas with God's love and renewal.

CHAPTER ONE

POSITION FOR RECOVERY!

It's Time To Take Your Position!

7 want to declare this over you right now. Receive this as a prophetic word. **"You will recover! God will restore!"** Let this be your declaration and declare right now: *"I will recover! God will restore!"* *Take a moment right now and declare this over your life!*

There's not a person alive who hasn't at one time or another experienced the deep pain and feelings of loss, whether it was the death of a loved one, a marital break down, rebellious children, financial pressure or health issues. We all have had to survive those crazy and painful seasons when we could have, and should have but we didn't! Sometimes our loss is because of our decisions. No matter how hard we try to act like we didn't have a choice, deep down inside - where no one gets to see - we know we are to blame for some of our losses.

There's something to be said about the mercies of God. God wrote repentance into the equation because He knew we were flawed. God knew we would disobey, rebel and do it our way at times. There is a verse that puts chills down my spine. It is Proverbs 14:12; *"There is a way that seems right unto a man, but in the end leads to destruction (death)."*

God has more mercy in His plan than He has judgment. I know this may sound like a honey gospel, but the truth is that God wants to work with us. He wants to restore us more than He desires to destroy us. Religion has made God out to be a robotic and mechanical God that only does it one way. I see a completely different kind of GOD when I read the Bible.

I see a God that loves more than hates and forgives faster than He wants to judge. I see Him as loving, kind, caring and reaching to us as a warm and protective father. God loves us and always provides an opportunity for repentance. When we repent, God is able and quick to stop the crisis, stop the trauma and reverse the consequences as fast as they were permitted.

God is a God of recovery. He's a God of restoration. I don't care how bad you've done it or how bad you're doing it. All you have to do is confess your sins and tell God you're sorry and accept His Son, Jesus, as the bridge between you and Him.

MEANINGS OF THE WORD RECOVERY:

1. The regaining of, or possibility of regaining, something lost or taken away.
2. The restoration or return to health.
3. The restoration or return to any former and better state of condition.
4. Something that is gained in recovery.
5. An improvement in the economy marking the end of a recession or decline.
6. The obtaining of a right to something by verdict or judgment.

RECOVERY MEANS MORE

I like these various definitions because I believe that when God is involved in my recovery, all these meanings are involved in the process. ***Get excited; you are living in the time of recovery!*** Understand that when God is involved with your recovery, He makes the **enemy add interest to your loss**. You don't just recover, you recover with gain.

"...Yet when he (the thief or enemy) is found, he must restore sevenfold; He may have to give up all the substance of his house." Proverbs 6:31 NKJV

No matter what you have done, when you discover that the enemy was behind your loss, you can claim this as your recovery verse through Christ Jesus, even after a bad decision. God can reverse the wrong and make it right. He calls this forgiveness and mercy. We activate the law of mercy when we repent and His mercy is two-fold.

First, God's mercy is new every morning. *"This I recall to my mind, therefore I have hope. Through the Lord's mercies we are not consumed, Because His compassions fail not. They are new every morning; Great is your faithfulness. "The Lord is my portion," says my soul, "Therefore I hope in Him!"" Lamentations 3:21-24 NKJV*

No matter what you did yesterday, when you wake up, God has brand new mercies for you. I love this about the Lord. He believes and hopes in me every morning. God gives me new mercies every morning. He waits on me to repent from yesterday's failures and mistakes and to decide to change. Mercy is defined as [1]*clemency: leniency and compassion shown toward offenders by a person or agency charged with administering justice…*

Only God has the right to judge your mistakes and when we plead with Him, He's a God of mercy! God gives us a day of clemency, leniency and, above all, compassion. No one can show mercy or walk in forgiveness with anyone until they possess and move in the heart of compassion.

This is hard for humans who have to live in a cruel and cynical world, where everyone is competing to outdo others in life and relationships. Thank God He is not like us! We are to strive to be like Him by forgiving those who hurt us and living our lives in the realm of compassion… His compassion!

I must confess that I struggle with this one. I can be so uncompassionate at times. My heart aches to be more like Christ. I am so weak in this area of my life. Competition can be my greatest enemy. This stems from my wounds of rejection, insecurities and a low self-image. Maybe you're thinking, how does a person who writes books, travels, ministers on television and pastor's a church have all these in his mind? I have to fight them every day. What I do doesn't help who I am. What I am has to be forged through Christ. What I do is my duty. What I am becoming is because my self-image is now in HIM! Christ! You have to die to self to develop a healthy self-image. I have decided to build my self-worth in Christ. I AM because HE WAS!

Every day brings brand new decisions and God wants to give you brand new mercy. He doesn't carry over from yesterday's stupidity.

His mercies are everlasting. *"For the Lord is good; his mercy is everlasting; and his truth endureth to all generations"* *Psalms 100:5 KJV.* God has no end, thus His mercy has no end. Everlasting means forever and ever. No end means that mercy was around before you and I were around and mercy will be here after you and I are gone. Mercy transcends time.

RULES FOR MERCY

God's mercy has qualifications attached to it. *"But the mercy of the Lord is from everlasting to everlasting upon them that fear him, and his righteousness unto children's children: To such as keep his covenant, and to those that remember his commandments to do them. The Lord hath prepared his throne in the heavens; and his kingdom ruleth over all." Psalms 103:17-19 KJV*

You don't activate His mercy just because you're alive.

> **Repentance is the Requirement for Mercy**

You activate His mercy when you decide to give up who you are and obey and live by His laws. All of God's laws have different rewards. Repentance is the key to mercy!

Laws for the reward of Mercy

1. ***Fear Him***: This doesn't mean to be afraid of Him, but to reverence Him. This word, fear, can really be called HONOR. When we honor God we trust Him. We obey Him. We make Him our source and not man.

   Honor is the key to access. A better way to say this is that honor is the law to access. Honor gives you the reward for God's access and, that access, is given to you because of mercy.

2. ***Be a Covenant Keeper***: You will not receive mercy if you

break God's Covenant. It would be very prudent for you to learn and study all you can about the Covenant and your Covenant rights. I have a 15 CD teaching series that I did on the subject of Covenant. You can order it on my website: *www.bishopgrillo.com*. This series will help you claim your Covenant rights and to live them out for Covenant rewards.

3. ***Remember and Obey God's Laws:*** Commands are not the same as covenant. A covenant is a contract between two parties. A law or command is activated by obedience. All of God's laws have different rewards attached to them; for instance, the law of confessing His Son, Jesus, as Lord and Savior gives us the reward of eternal life in heaven.

MERCY IS WHY GOD RESTORES

God isn't about taking, **He's about releasing**. He's about recovering what we've lost. This understanding can empower you to receive God's restoration.

The children of Israel witnessed firsthand miracles, signs and wonders in the wilderness. Manna, or bread, was fresh on the ground each morning, meat rained out of heaven, water flowed from a rock and bitter waters turned sweet. If that wasn't enough, God was with them as a cloud by day and a pillar of fire by night.

All these signs and yet they limited God because of their unbelief. They couldn't stretch their faith beyond what they could see in the natural. God had destined them for the Promised Land, but they had settled for the comfort of just enough and were unwilling to believe for more.

God desires to give to release His power, His blessings and His grace. If you're not experiencing release whose fault is it? In case you don't get it, *it may be your fault!*

OUTPOURING IS ABOUT INCREASE

Increase is the only proof that God's Spirit is poured out. Outpouring is about increase. When the Spirit touched the people in the book of Acts, they experienced an outpouring of the Holy Spirit and the church increased that day by three thousand souls. You will experience increase when God touches your life.

We need to shift our thinking. God is not a mechanical, robotic being that sits on a big throne with long, white hair and a white cape waiting to judge all of us. God always identified Himself as a God of lineage; a God that wants to be known for His kindness and love. He wants us to know that He cares for us and that He is here for us. He's the father you never had, a counselor and friend that sticks closer than a brother. He's not sitting in heaven waiting for us to mess up. We will mess up! He's there with arms open and a kind, warm smile on His face saying, *"I know you fell. I know you messed up. Come to me all you who are heavy and sad; I will give you sanctuary."*

Other Laws to Consider:

1. Adaptability: the Law for Change
2. Attitude: the Law for Access
3. Seed: the Law for Increase
4. Change: the Law for Growth
5. Words: the Law for Life or Death
6. "IF": the Law for Exchange
7. Honor: the Law for Access
8. Honor Your Parents: The Law for a Less Stressed Life
9. Favor: The Law for Seasons
10. Discomfort: the Law for Transition
11. Praise: The Law for Attracting God
12. Obedience: the Law for Miracles
13. Expectation: the Law that Pleases God

CHAPTER TWO

EVERY SEASON HAS AN END

7 believe that everything happens for a reason. I believe that in everything God schedules a start and an end. No season is meant to last forever. In the natural, seasons usually last three months. We experience four seasons every year; winter, spring, summer and fall. The same is true in the spiritual. Sometimes we do experience prolonged seasons in our lives, but no matter what we are facing the season is scheduled to end.

I believe that in everything God schedules a **"turn around"** anointing. He can turn every set back into a comeback! The crisis is not sent to break you down, but to build you up to be stronger and last longer on the earth.

ARE YOU EARNING A LIVING OR DESIGNING A LIFE?

Have you ever noticed in the gospel of Matthew, Jesus' genealogy starts with Abraham and not Adam?

"The book of the generation of Jesus Christ, the son of David, the son of Abraham." Matthew 1:1

"So all the generations from Abraham to David are fourteen generations; and from David until the carrying away into Babylon are fourteen generations; and from the carrying away into Babylon unto Christ are fourteen generations." Matthew 1:17

We can't fully grasp a true understanding of this genealogical account if we don't understand the primary purpose of Jesus and how it relates to the Word of God.

Notice in verse seventeen the equal comparison to fourteen generations. Fourteen times three equals forty-two. I don't think this is accidental. Job chapter forty-two gives us our first clue into God's primary purpose and what He really wants to do.

*"And the **LORD restored** Job's losses when he prayed for his friends... Indeed the **LORD gave** Job **twice as much** as he had before... Each one gave him a piece of silver and each a ring of gold. **Now the LORD blessed the latter days of Job more than his beginning...**" Job 42:10 -12*

God had a plan to replace Adam with the lineage of the father of faith, Abraham. God wanted to make us aware that His purpose is to restore - not according to our works or actions - but according to our faith. So it's befitting that He started Jesus' genealogy with Abraham and not Adam.

God's focus is to restore what we've lost. We are imprinted through religious teaching that the only people who need restoration are those who live in blatant sin and rebellion. This is not true. The power of God is for all of us. This power isn't just to rescue us from a sinful lifestyle but to restore us from something even greater than sin; something that imprisons us all and blocks us from taking our positions as sons of God.

IT IS IMPORTANT HOW WE APPROACH SCRIPTURE.

The view you take over the Word of God will decide how you process to your turn around moment.

You cannot approach the Bible as if it is an ordinary book with an ordinary story to tell. Almost everything in the Bible hinges on the unusual and the extraordinary. The first unusual thing is that *THE WORD OF GOD IS ALIVE!*

The Word of God is alive; it's not a history book. The same Power that was working in the lives of people thousands of years ago is still working in our lives today!

There's a story in the Bible about a boy named David. This young man decided to face a giant named Goliath. Goliath was defiling the name of the Lord. David became stirred in his spirit to defend the Lord's Honor! He faced odds greater than his abilities and greater than his stature as a boy. Goliath was at least twelve feet tall.

David faced his crisis and defeated this giant with a slingshot and a rock. The same God that delivered David can also deliver us (1 Samuel 17: 1-58).

There's another story in the Bible that comes to mind in the book of Daniel chapter one. It is a story about three Hebrew guys named Shadrach, Meshach and Abednego. We don't know a lot about them, but we do know they loved God and continually put their faith in Him. The Bible tells us that God gave them greater wisdom than their peers. Wisdom comes from spending time with God and His Word. Obviously, they were familiar with God's miracles and promises throughout the Old Testament.

These boys refused to bow to an image created by the King of Babylon. The King of Babylon decreed that any time the music was played during the day, everyone was to bow and worship a golden image of the king. Those who wouldn't obey would be put to death by fire. One day the music sounded and all the people fell to their faces except these three Hebrew boys. The king saw them standing and because he liked them gave them a second opportunity. He asked them, *"Didn't you hear the music?"* Their answer was, *"Yes we did! But we are not going to bow."* The story goes on to say that this king put all three of the men into the fire, but only those who threw them in were burned up.

We don't know how but we know God did it. The story goes on to say that when the king looked into the furnace he saw one more than was thrown in. The fourth image appeared to be like GOD! God delivered them from the furnace and the fire.

The same God then is the same God today. He will enter the fire of your tribulation and reverse its scheduled destruction. He will turn things around in a moment!

"Man shall not live by bread alone, but by every word that proceeds out of the mouth of God." Matthew 4:4

The Word of God is alive. It is filled with story after story that proves we serve a "Turn-Around" God.

There is no word in the Bible that means **coincidence**. Coincidence means *a striking occurrence of two or more events at one time apparently by mere chance*.

Every story has a purpose and a deeper meaning than just to entertain us. Things just don't happen! The same is true in our lives. God is at work behind all of our craziness. I believe God has orchestrated things in our lives to help us, train us and grow us. In the end, His will is going to be supreme in my life and in yours.

NEXT MOVE IN OUR SPIRITUAL PURSUIT

"So Abram departed, as the LORD had spoken unto him..." **Genesis 12:4.** Abram didn't leave because he was bored and ready to travel. The Lord told Abram to depart, to leave where he was and come out from among his family and follow Him. There was a reason this happened.

God moved from His silence and wanted to intervene in man's affairs. Abram had to be willing to hear in order for God to help! To fully understand what Abram was departing from, we must go back a few more chapters in Genesis.

"And Cush begat Nimrod: he began to be a mighty one in the earth. He was a mighty hunter before the LORD: wherefore it is said, Even as Nimrod the mighty hunter before the LORD." **Genesis 10: 8-9**

Cush had a son named Nimrod. Nimrod was a mighty hunter. Nimrod created a system that put men in bondage to an enslaved mindset. We must dive deeper into this story in Genesis to fully understand why God sent Jesus and why His primary focus is to restore, bring recovery and transform us.

Let's break this down into the following words:

1. Babel
2. Nimrod

3. Mighty
4. Hunter
5. Tower

Babel: Strong's Hebrew number 894.
Hebrew '**Confusion**', Akkadian and Sumerian *'Gate of God'*.

"The beginning of his kingdom was Babylon..." Genesis 10:10

Notice that no end is ever mentioned to Nimrod's kingdom. It has a start that continues relentlessly on throughout scripture, infiltrating the people of God and causing them to stumble. The name means **confusion! This system always creates confusion.**

In *Joshua 7:21*, the word "Babel" stood for a beautiful mantle from Shinar (the plain in which Babylon was located) that was instrumental in tempting Achan to disobey the Word of God when the Israelites were in the process of annihilating Jericho. It was a desire for a worldly item that led one of God's people away from obedience to the revealed *"will"* of God.

At one time, Satan had his seat in that same geographical location as the prophecy of *Isaiah* speaks, which is directly against the **'king of Babylon'.** It was Babylon that finally took God's people into exile.

When the Jews found themselves far removed from the Promised Land, they took to heart the Lord's words through Jeremiah to seek the land's welfare. They became entangled in the Babylonian ways and did not **wholeheartedly** return to the land when they were granted permission under King Cyrus. Repeated warnings to His people, concerning the removal of themselves *from Babylon* so that God could judge the nation, went unheeded and He withheld His hand.

In *Revelation 17:5*, Babylon is called *"mother of harlots"* and of earth's abominations; the one that is responsible for slaying God's servants, whether that be the removing of physical or spiritual life. **It is the source of what is abominable in God's eyes and it rules over the kings of the earth.**

Babylon began its history under **Nimrod** and remains the name given to *a system that is actively opposed to the will of God on the earth*.

Babel/Babylon was the beginning of man's organized rebellion against God and His divine plan for man. It is the beginning of a **dominance** that draws its adherents away from following after the ways and purposes of God. It is a system that uses religious words to enslave the minds of people in such a way that they become confused and blind to real truth. Nimrod is the mighty leader of the satanic system that people follow and when they do, they become enslaved to earning a living but not designing a life.

Nimrod

The name 'Nimrod' (Strong's Hebrew number 5248) perhaps comes from a Hebrew root and means **'rebel,'** but the exact derivative of the name is by no means certain.

Names meant things in the Bible and were not mere idle labels that could be laid aside and ignored. If Nimrod's name meant **'rebel'** then it gives us insight into his character, a life of rebellion. Some have stated that his name had two meanings, like a two-sided coin. Nimrod's name has two meanings. The first meaning is, **"I will go up"** and the other is, **"You will go down"**. Thereby Nimrod's system was birthed through rebellion.

You will find yourselves in a never-ending cycle of rebellion to God's original plan if you buy into this system; a system for man to be empowered, to rule his own life and not be caught up in slavery and work. While we are earning a living, the "Nimrodites" are going up and we are going down. Their wealth and living is based on our hours, our lives and our families.

Mighty

"[Nimrod] began to be a warrior on the earth" (I Chronicles 1:10, Genesis 10:8)

Nimrod began to be a 'warrior' or 'mighty one.' The scripture does not say that he **was** but that he **began to be**. Like his kingdom, which is spoken of in Genesis chapter ten, his reign as a warrior begins but it has no end.

In similar language the Bible speaks about all that Jesus *began* to do and teach, meaning that His earthly ministry was only the start of what He continued to do through His followers after He ascended into heaven.

This calls for a rethink in our interpretation of the passage. Nimrod is more than just a historical figure who laid the foundation of his own kingdom; he was an instigator of the ***movement of rebellion against the rule of God*** (as Nimrod's name suggests).

Therefore, in a passage previously mentioned above, the prophecy directed at the 'king of Babylon' (who is Nimrod, in Genesis) speaks about Satan.

Now, we see Satan's strategy in the Garden of Eden was to pull God's creation away from a pure relationship with Him with deceit and lies. After the flood, his purpose was to unite man together in a movement that is **in rebellion against God's purposes.**

Hunter: Manipulator

Nimrod is spoken of as being both a hunter and a king (by inference of him having a kingdom), but these two characteristics are incompatible. He wants to rule like God, but can't be a ruler and a hunter. Ungers writes *'Whereas a hunter gratifies himself at the expense of his victim, the shepherd expends himself for the good of the subjects of his care.'*

There, Nimrod was not, nor ever would be, God's choice of a leader. He is nothing like Jesus!

Nimrod's hunting abilities were aimed at men. He hunted them to bring them under his own sovereignty and control. This was where his own strength lay, not in his prowess of catching game, but in capturing men to do his own will. Nimrod was a **manipulator** and a type of the anti-Christ. He was the first of those we have seen throughout history like Nero, Napoleon, Hitler and so on.

Satan, like Nimrod, is a hunter trying to be king and not a shepherd who is king. Look below to see the distinction between Jesus the Shepherd King verses Satan the Hunter King.

1. A **Hunter/ King** rules at the expense of his victim and this is what Satan does when he captures men to do his will. As it says in *Isaiah 14:17,* Satan '...did not let his prisoners go home', meaning that his rule was not one of liberty but of continual bondage.
2. A **Shepherd/ King** is what Jesus is. This is first revealed in Genesis 12:1, *"Now Abram, come out from among them. So Abram departed."* He followed the voice of a Shepherd-King. When He comes down, men will go up!

Nimrod is the system where those who are influenced by it, use its power to hunt out and capture men, to establish its own dominion of rebellion against God throughout the entire earth. It is masked in the name "corporate" or "capitalism" that is solely used to enslave people into a minimum wage lifestyle. This keeps people from ever fully reaching their God given potential. It is Satan's intention to use this system to destroy mankind. He doesn't do it himself, but he uses men to do his will as it destroys and undermines both God's creation and will. We must understand that Satan was defeated through the blood of Jesus and by His resurrection. Our warfare is not with him, but with our own desires and lofty thinking. [ii]

"For though we live in the world, we do not wage war as the world does. The weapons we fight with are not the weapons of the world. On the contrary, they have divine power to demolish strongholds. We demolish arguments and every pretension that sets itself up against the knowledge of God, and we take captive every thought to make it obedient to Christ." 2 Corinthians 10:3-5

THE BATTLE TO WIN COMES FROM WITHIN

I believe we've been taught too long to focus our spiritual warfare against a fallen enemy. This enemy is what we call devils, demons, and yes, the main one himself, Lucifer. The truth is that this enemy is defeated. The only power that they have is in the attachment of our own desires and wants that do not line up to the Word of God and the truth of that Word, Jesus.

The biggest warfare we face is in our minds, our heads, and *"powers of high places"*. These powers aren't flying over your head or in your room. They are in your **thoughts and minds**. You give your thoughts power to create, to perform and to change the atmosphere in your life when you give them focus. Yes, we live in the world, but we do not wage war as the world does. We do not use our flesh and emotions to combat what we are facing. We are supposed to use the Word of God. We are not to use what someone has told us through denominational persuasion and influences. We are to use the truth of God's Word. We are to use it as it is revealed to us through our own understanding. When it becomes a part of us, it will then speak out of us through our own inner man and not through our emotional man.

Let's look at a scriptural verse that we all know and, I believe, misuse:

"We use God's mighty weapons, not worldly weapons, to knock down the strongholds of human reasoning and to destroy false arguments." 2 Corinthians 10:4 NLT

This warfare, this high place is in our heads. The mind is where the greatest warfare is taking place; not over your head as much as in your head. I'm not advocating that there's no Devil, or even demons. That would be unscriptural. What I am stating is that we spend far too much time fighting demons and the Devil when by scriptural understanding He's been dealt with, defeated and stripped of all power, by and through Jesus Christ.

"In this way, he disarmed the spiritual rulers and authorities. He shamed them publicly by his victory over them on the cross." *Colossians 2:15 NLT*

Paul was always conscious of this warfare. At the end of his life's journey he said, *"I have fought a good fight, I have finished my course, I have kept the faith." 2 Timothy 4:7*

Paul's warfare consisted of two areas:

1. In the mind.

2. Over our faith! Notice Ephesians 6:11 says to *"Put on the whole armor of God"*. Faith is simply defined as 'what a person believes'. Where does this live? In our minds and in our persuasions.

Where does this rebellion live and find its power? Not around us, but within us. This is why Paul said that greater is He that is in us than that which is around us (paraphrased). We are defeated in battle when we focus more on our thoughts, emotions, feelings and wants. The Bible is to be used as a cleansing agent for the mind, to renew it and realign your thinking back to God's way instead of man's way.

Nimrod and his system end in the lake of fire **(Revelation 20:10)** where it will be punished forever. The spirit of Nimrod will be banished from the earth along with the Babylonian system over which it rules.

Tower of Babel

"...this is only the beginning of what [mankind] will do." Genesis 11:6

While it is impossible to say one way or the other, Nimrod is so inextricably bound up with the Babylonian's foundation that we would not be going too far to see into the incident of Genesis

11:1-9, another aspect of Nimrod's kingdom that had implications throughout the course of subsequent history. This appears to be connected with him.

The men that came together in the plain of Shinar had three purposes (Genesis 11:4):

1. The building of a city-The city was a place that they all intended to live in.
2. The building of a tower-The tower was a place that they all intended to worship in and earthly reputation was what they wanted corporately. (The Scripture says that they wanted to make 'a name' and not 'names' for themselves.)
3. Making a name for themselves-Making a name for themselves is the only sign that they were being led by their own image and not the image of God. Here's where we see the first glimpse of religion; when we attempt to do something using God as our focus, but our intent is to make a name for ourselves.

At this time, there was only one language on the earth which meant that there was a natural unity among all mankind. This was God's provision.

This doesn't matter to the mind of humanism. Fallen men under the direction of Nimrod **attempt** to bring themselves into a position of unity that is stronger than that which already existed (*"Behold, they are one people..."* Genesis **11:6a)**. The natural unity of language that they had was exploited to produce a unity among themselves that God had not intended to be achieved. They are missing it by using God's provision for their own selfish gain and name. Doesn't that sound a bit familiar?

God's plan was attached to His command...*"Be fruitful and multiply and fill the earth..."* (Genesis 9:1). What Nimrod and his followers were doing was trying to put off this command and settle, by attempting to establish themselves in one area. (Genesis 11:2 - *'they settled there'* and Genesis 11:4 - *'let us build'.)* Even in what appears to be a noble cause, there is rebellion lurking behind the scenes. When we attempt to add our wishes and plans to God's intended instructions, no matter how noble it may appear, to God it is disobedience. This decision will always end up in confusion and distraction.

Fake Nobility

Notice that the building of a tower *"...with its top in the heavens..."* is an attempt at **religious** unity (Genesis 11:4). In ancient times, the high places were places of *sacrifice so that the tower would have been a place where each one of them performed various religious rites*.

"Having its top in the heavens" is a way of saying that they were attempting "to reach up to God and to ascend back into a relationship with Him through their own efforts. The cross speaks to us of God's descent to man and the importance to restore ourselves into covenant relationship with God. See how this system is still alive today? Self-righteousness is a plague against what God's true intent is for mankind.

Even though their reach...their focus...and their attempt is to heaven, God still has to come down to see what's going on because they fall too far short of their target **(Genesis 11:5).**

God is concerned for mankind, taking an active part in human affairs by descending to earth to witness men's deeds. He did this again before judging Sodom and Gomorrah (Genesis 18:21), when He came to deliver His people out of Egypt (Exodus 3:8), when He gave commandments to Israel (Exodus 19:11,20) and ultimately, when He came to earth to secure an eternal redemption on behalf of His people (Ephesians 4:9-10, John 1:1,14).

It is said of Satan, the king of Babylon, *You said in your heart "I will ascend to heaven; above the stars of God I will set my throne on high; I will sit on the mount of assembly in the far north; I will ascend above the heights of the clouds, I will make myself like the Most High"* (Isaiah 14:13-14). This shows connection to this passage in Genesis. Satan's intention was to establish a place from which he would challenge the rule of God.

Man's attempt at unity brings confusion (Genesis 11:9). God imparted different languages to the community so that the unity that they had been aiming for was destroyed and their fear of being scattered over the face of the earth (Genesis 11:4) is exactly what they end up reaping (Genesis 11:9)! (Notice Genesis 10:25 which appears to relate to this incident - ...**for in his days the earth was divided**).

'The tower of the gateway of God' proved to be 'the tower of confusion'. By comparison of the two different origins of the name for Babylon, the Hebrew derivative is a direct comment on what Babylon was supposed to be.

The tower of man's attempts to reach God results only in chaos and fails to meet its objective. Man's religion does not have a Divine origin but an earthly one that seeks the Divine union and blessing upon the things that it wants to do. But God is the originator of all true spirituality.

Nimrod is the **'rebel'** who established **'confusion'** in the earth by claiming that his kingdom brought the 'gateway of God' to man.

STOP RACISM... COMPETION... JEALOUSIES!

The end of nationalism, tribalism and patriotism is only possible in Christ as a work that God brings about (Galatians 3:28; Ephesians 2:14-16). Just as a diversity of tongues brought about confusion and disunity to mankind, so a diversity of tongues inspired by the Holy Spirit brings unity (Acts 2:1-4, 44-45).

We must beware lest we are carried along on the wave of ecumenicalism *(this simply means relating to the worldwide Christian church)* thinking that by uniting with religions that appear similar to Christianity, we are uniting for strength. **Far from it!** A religious union will only produce confusion and will ultimately result in destruction. The only 'unity' is that which is imparted by the Holy Spirit as a gift of God through conversion and immersion in the Holy Spirit. In aiming to unite men and women together in Christ, we are aiming for the target that they might be converted by God to serve Jesus, and be brought into unity by the power of the Holy Spirit. It does not come through religious tolerance or compromise.

It is difficult to determine if there will be one world ruler or not. It may be that the false leader is a ruler over a large proportion of the globe or over the most powerful and influential of the nations (as the emperors of Rome were). One thing is certain - ultimately it will not bring a lasting unity but disaster, just as man's first attempt at unity ended up with confusion (II Thessalonians 2:3-4,8). Notice that 'rebellion' is spoken of which is the meaning of the name Nimrod. In addition, every existing religion is superseded by that one individual who claims supremacy over all thereby bringing religious syncretism, which the construction of the tower was at the first attempt of achieving.[iii]

God Says, "Abram, come out! Abram Depart!"

In Genesis 12, what did God call Abram out of? He was in the crowds of those who were attempting false unity and false religions. Abram was standing in the crowds of those who were being influenced by Nimrod. Remember, this is the system where *"one goes up, while the masses serving this system go down"*. It is where we've built the word "corporate". Think about it! People work 40 to 50 hours a week at a minimum wage. I was in the UK and asked my driver what the minimum wage was there. His reply was, *"We call it slave wage here"*. Wow! So here's our life; we work for income that barely meets our needs while those we work for keep going up. Our finances don't change and eventually we retire. What do we retire with? We retire with enough to scratch out a minimal existence. How can this be God's way? It's not! So God calls us out just as HE called out Abram.

"Therefore, come out from among unbelievers, and separate yourselves from them, says the LORD. Don't touch their filthy things, and I will welcome you..." 2 Corinthians 6:17 NLT

Just like Abram, we are commanded to come out and be separate. Follow the voice of God, serve Him and touch not or believe in this system of false religion and status quo living. We are to come out and walk by our faith. God said He would receive us and welcome us. Just like it was for Abram, so it will be for us.

In Revelation, God calls His people to *'come out of here'*. This time He promises destruction and judgment upon the Babylonian system that is opposed to His will (Revelation 18:2).

LET US BE WARNED!

If like the Jews in exile, our lives are so integrated into the present world systems, then when God executes judgment upon them **for our benefit** we will not respond with the Hallelujah chorus of Revelation 19:1-3, but we will fall with it. Any world system that pulls us away from serving God must be removed from ourselves.

Although there is a freedom in Christ, it is not a freedom that is licentiousness, an excessive liberty (Jude 4) that causes us to become entangled in pursuits that rob us of the life of God (II Timothy 2:4).

So this is why the genealogy of Jesus Christ started with Abram. Abram departed! Abram represents the spirit of faith. He is the father of faith. We must do what he did to get what he got. He received the promise from God to be blessed!

I command your life, in the name of Jesus, to be set free and to understand the primary purpose of God, which purpose is to redeem us from the curse of fallen man; to be redeemed and restored to our original status on the earth, and subdue, have dominion and multiply! Do you receive it?

CHAPTER THREE

MOMENTUM IS SHIFTING FOR YOUR RESTORATION!

*M*omentum is a powerful ingredient to recovering all! There must be an understanding that movement doesn't necessarily mean you have momentum. One of the greatest deceptions in life is to believe you are making progress and succeeding just because you are moving. I have witnessed many people who are moving and look busy but never get anywhere. They move to the altar but stay the same. They move to and from new jobs but they're always in the same financial crisis. I've watched people move from one relationship to another but are never happy. Movement means nothing unless you're making progress.

Movement without arrival is nothing more than driving on an endless highway to nowhere. It's like driving in a cul-de-sac; one way in and no way out. Many people in our churches assume that they are creating spiritual momentum because they go to church and read their Bible.

Sadly, movement is not momentum. Of course you can't have momentum without movement, but you can most certainly be moving and have no momentum.

What is momentum and what generates it? Momentum is a force that pushes you…it is the power behind movement. A ship in full motion has such momentum that if you cut off all power it will continue to move forward for one mile before it comes to a complete stop. Why? It has momentum behind it; a force stronger than the opposition in front of it. That opposition takes one mile to affect the motion or movement forward progress of the ship. Think about how powerful momentum is. The force behind you is stronger than the opposition that is attempting to hold you in place. Even when all power has stopped, you still have the force behind you pushing you through. This is why Satan hates believers who have momentum. Even when they seem to have lost power, they still experience tremendous breakthroughs. I want to stop right here and say….**PREPARE FOR YOUR**

MOMENTUM TO SHIFT. I believe that right now momentum is shifting in your favor.

The denser an object in movement is, the more power the momentum behind it will have. The heavier the object, the more momentum is created. For instance, I can throw a towel at a brick wall. No matter how hard and how fast I throw it, the towel lacks the weight necessary to create the momentum necessary to experience a breakthrough. Weight decides the potential of momentum. There's a scripture in the Bible that I believe explains this:

*"And there came a man of God, and spake unto the king of Israel, and said, Thus saith the Lord, Because the Syrians have said, **The Lord is God of the hills, but he is not God of the valleys,** therefore will I deliver all this great multitude into thine hand, and ye shall know that I am the Lord."* *1 Kings 20:28*

Notice that the enemy assumes that we can only praise and act like we are winners when we are living on the mountain. Where does the enemy get this assumption? After studying God's people, the enemy noticed a trend or pattern that the people of God were only excited when they were in the high places of life.

Many have revealed this same trait today. They only give when they have more than they need. They only support the church when they are feeling good about life. Many only attend church when things are great but quit when things are bad. When I wake up on Sunday morning to rainy and gloomy weather, I already know that church attendance is going to be low. Why? Because I believe people have a hard time functioning in their joy and faith during stormy weather. This plays over into their spiritual life as well.

The enemy said in this passage of scripture that the Lord is only God in the high times of life, but He is not Lord in the valley. However, God sent a man of God to declare to the king that He would deliver His people out of the hand of the enemy. I declare to you that we will fight the enemy in the valley, and in that valley we will beat him down.

This is why I believe God doesn't always respond when we expect Him too. Sometimes He delays so that we can experience the valley. What good is being God, All-Powerful, All Knowing and Almighty if you can't show off how powerful you really are? It is in the valley where we learn how great our God is. If you think about it, almost all of the battles in the Bible were fought in valleys. *David beat Goliath in a valley... Jericho is in a valley... The last battle, Armageddon, will be fought in a valley.*

Momentum is created when you win in the valley. When you come out of the lowest place of your life the winner, you create such momentum that the rest of the enemy's opposition is easily beaten. The force behind you becomes greater than the opposition in front of you.

Who can threaten Jesus? The enemy has no more power to threaten someone who survived death's final blow and rose from the ashes of the grave.

One of the ways Satan stops momentum is to build such a crisis in front of you that you will not even attempt to enter into conflict or try to fight back. Jesus knew the devastation of the cross, but he looked past the momentary affliction to the joy of living, after the enemy was defeated. Jesus used the eyes of revelation to stay focused on the victory instead of the pain of the valley.

"Looking unto Jesus the author and finisher of our faith; who for the joy that was set before him endured the cross, despising the shame, and is set down at the right hand of the throne of God." Hebrew 12:2 KJV

Don't Allow Your Situation To Define You

When you're facing a situation you have to maintain your faith no matter what. Satan is going to use anything he can to persuade you not to believe in your future. His whole warfare tactic is to scare you bad enough that you will not even attempt to enter battle.

"And Benhadad the king of Syria gathered all his host together: and there were thirty and two kings with him, and horses, and chariots; and he went up and besieged Samaria, and warred against it. And he sent messengers to Ahab king of Israel into the city, and said unto him, Thus saith Benhadad, Thy silver and thy gold is mine; thy wives also and thy children, even the goodliest, are mine. And the king of Israel answered and said, My lord, O king, according to thy saying, I am thine, and all that I have." I Kings 20: 1-4

Anything Uncontested Will Flourish

What really gets me here that I seem to relate to is how easily Ahab fell into the trap of what he saw. Not one arrow has been fired. Not one encounter with the enemy has been attempted. Think for a moment; all Ahab saw was the power and size of his situation and he couldn't even fathom attempting to fight.

This is Satan's greatest warfare against believers. All he has to do is put a mountain in our way, a situation that looks so large and intimidating, that we will immediately lose our focus and passion and become persuaded that there is no use. There's no way we can overcome, overpower or even make a dent into this crisis.

I have a prophecy for you today. You will only succeed in the Kingdom when you receive this word: **warfare is your destiny.** Oh yeah! I'm telling you the truth! The situation isn't going to go away just because you don't fight. It will get bigger and worse. *Anything uncontested flourishes*! I will speak more on this in the next chapter.

> **Feelings Are Real. Feelings Have Power.**

You must fight the urge to talk about the situation you are facing. So many people spend countless hours and days discussing their problems with family, friends and co-workers. The situation doesn't get solved; it only gets bigger. Our continuous conversation about the problem makes the problem become unconquerable. Our ears are hearing our own words of defeat and those words are defeating us. The words you speak will give the situation power of control over your mind and feelings. I don't care what people say. *Feelings are powerful*. Feelings can be hard to overcome. If we can't change the way we feel we may not ever get out of the situation.

The mind will buy into our own discussions. We have to start putting words to our faith. It is so important that we look past the situation into our faith and future. We need to find someplace where we can point our faith to and say this is where God spoke to me. This is where I can prove that this situation isn't supposed to destroy me. I've been anointed for this, not that! WOW! What a thought! What a great sermon title! "This. Not that…" You must not let the situation define your feelings. Fight the temptation to allow the loss, the pain and the mountain you are facing to create words of agreement to it.

*"For verily I say unto you, That whosoever **shall say unto this mountain**, Be thou removed, and be thou cast into the sea; and **shall not doubt in his heart, but shall believe that those things which he saith shall come to pass**; he shall have whatsoever he **saith**. Therefore I say unto you, What things so ever ye desire, when ye pray, believe that ye receive them, and ye shall have them." Mark 11: 23,24*

CHAPTER FOUR

WARFARE IS YOUR DESTINY!

*Y*ou need to understand this one thing about the Kingdom of God. Warfare is a clue that you have destiny. Nothing comes to you in the Kingdom without opposition and warfare.

Battle is the seed for territory!

To experience a turnaround you have to be willing to fight. Warfare will not leave. Conflict will not go away. You can't pray it away or sow a seed to get rid of it. You can't wait it away. If you want to enter the season of promise, you simply have to learn how to fight!

We are Living Our Thoughts!

I'm not just talking about fighting devils. I'm speaking of every level of warfare; from the spirit world to your will, mind and emotions. The most warfare you will ever experience over your promised future will not be a devil or demon. It will be over your own will and mind. The battlefield for your tomorrow is in your head. Your thinking will decide your living. The Bible is clear on this subject.

The life that we live is created by the thoughts that we think.

"As a man thinks so is he…" Proverb 23: 7

Dr. Tal Ben-Shahar is a professor at Harvard who teaches a popular class on **Happiness** and has written a book entitled **Happier**. His main conclusion is that it is not **external circumstances that determine** a person's level of happiness, but rather, **it is their frame of mind**. Here's a short list of what determines one's happiness:

1. How the person thinks.

2. How the person talks.
3. How the person acts.

When I read this, my mind immediately went to the scripture, *"For as he thinketh in his heart, so is he..." Proverbs 23:7*

If you read the entire passage, you will find that the scripture actually refers to a person who is acting in an evil way.

- If we think evil, we will become evil.
- If we think trouble, we will become troubled.
- If we think good, we will become good.
- If we think happiness, we will become happy.
- If we allow our mind to focus, our mind will produce the right emotions to create what it wants.

This definitely is a principle found in the Word of God, corroborated by psychological studies and by simple observations of the people around us. We've all seen it. We've all experienced it. The life we lead is created by our thoughts. If we want to improve our life we will **have to improve our thoughts**. I believe that our mind and our thought life are the first battlegrounds for change. It is here in the secret corridors of the mind where the battle rages the longest and the hardest. Change here and you will eventually change. We are the architects of our own lives and unwittingly create pain and suffering for ourselves due to the unconscious thoughts we focus on within. God created us. God has a preordained future for us, but that doesn't guarantee we will experience or enter that preordained plan. The children of Israel had been preordained for the Promised Land; a land flowing with wealth and increase. They were destined for it but never obtained it. Just because God has scheduled it, doesn't mean you will show up for the appointment. Many have missed their divine moments. Many have fallen short of their divine preordained promise; not because it wasn't scheduled and not because it wasn't theirs, but because they couldn't adapt from the mind of welfare to warfare! I don't know about you, but I assure you I don't want to miss my **"TURN-AROUND"**! I don't want to wander in the wilderness of defeat and drought because my mind kept wondering where I belonged and what I was supposed to do. You and I are to fight! We are to go and possess the land, not just enter it.

Every thought that you think creates the reality you are living in. If you see yourself as being in lack then you will be in lack. If you think about going after and gaining wealth, then wealth is what you will obtain. It is simple to manifest in your life whatever you desire. **Desire is a powerful key here**. What is desire? What is the proof of it? Pursuit! When you have desire, you have passion to pursue. What you are unwilling to pursue is a clue your mind hasn't been persuaded that it's worth your action. Many miss the things of God simply because they won't pursue them. Think about how many times you've said in your life that you wished or wanted something. Think about how many times you've heard someone else say it. My question is why?

> **"The Proof of Desire is Pursuit."**
> **Mike Murdock**

Why didn't they obtain those things that they said they wanted and even said they loved? They wouldn't pursue it. What I won't pursue is a clue to what I really don't desire. I say I love it, but my unwillingness to pursue it shows that all I am is words of empty feelings and false passions.

- A husband says he loves his wife, then he will prove that by pursuit.
- A father says he loves his children, then he will prove it by his pursuit of them. When he trades them off for something else, He is declaring that He loves them less than what he's trading them off to pursue.
- A wife says she loves her husband but pursues something else. She's proven that she loves something else more than him.

- People say they love God but they are hardly ever involved with the things of God. They hardly ever read His word. That's like giving your wife a card that you wrote powerful and beautiful words in for her, but when you give it to her she puts it down and says, "I'll read it later". Later turns into days and months. Would you really believe her words if she didn't show you by her actions to pursue? No you wouldn't! How do you think God is interpreting our actions in His church? Just a thought!

To win this warfare battle over the mind, you must train your mind to see it before you can receive it. Visualize it; see yourself as if you already are where you want to be or the state of well being you desire to be in. You must get it in your head, not a onetime thought here, but an everyday thought. Day after day you keep seeing it, feeling it, desiring it and pursuing it. Get it in your head and keep it there no matter what is going on around you. Believe the house you want is yours. See it decorated! Close your eyes and smell the candles you've lit in the room. See yourself there and you will eventually materialize it by your faith.

This is exactly what happened to my assistant, April and her husband, Ritchie. They found a house they wanted and made an offer on it. The offer was turned downed. So what did they do? They went and drove a stake in the yard of that house and declared that it was theirs. A year and half later the house was still on the market. They decided to make another offer and it was accepted. Now they live in that house. Every time I went in Ritchie's office, I would see a picture of that house on his screen saver. They never released that house from their minds. They always saw it as theirs. They never gave up in their desire or in their hearts. They waited on timing and worked their faith. They sowed seeds for it. Now they possess it. Their will produced their desire to pursue and now they have received it. This isn't just a formula for the few. It is for all of us who desire to walk in TURN-AROUND POWER! The same will happen for you, but you must be willing to fight for it. We must **fight** all negative thoughts and feelings within ourselves, and the external negative thoughts from even our friends and family. These only serve to feed our doubts.

DECLARATION FOR MY TURN AROUND!

Enemy of increase and change, listen now, listen up and listen long! I am a part of the Church of the Redeemed! I am called; I am anointed and appointed to possess the land of promise by God! I serve notice today: **No more!** *No more tributes... No more compromise... No more complaining... No more losses... No more pain and no more lack! For my God is a very present help in times of trouble. And He is present now! God has not given me a spirit of fear, but of love, power and of a sound mind! My God is in the midst of His people. I will not be moved! Enemy! No weapon formed against us will prosper! For My God is an all-consuming fire!* **Today I will stand and behold His Majesty!** *iv*

People are stuck in their wilderness unchanged for a reason! It's not God's plan nor is it His will. It wasn't His plan for Israel and it's not His plan for us.

8 REASONS THAT KEEP YOU IN THE WILDERNESS:

1. **REACTIONS:** Reactions can be deadly. Monitor your reactions to God's plans, God's instructions and even to God's leaders.
2. **DECISIONS:** Decisions decide most of what you're experiencing in life. Behind every decision is a consequence. The children of Israel made some real bad decisions. They decided to listen to wrong voices and allow others to speak against God's set man, Moses. The next time you make a decision, remember you didn't choose the decision, you actually chose the consequence behind it. Don't complain and become angry if you don't like where you are; you chose it. It was your decision. **Decisions decide your _____. (you fill in the blank)** Whatever word you put there - decisions decided it.

Put joy there, put wealth there! This is a powerful thought!

3. **ADAPTATION:** You will stay stuck in the circle of defeat, drought and failure (wilderness) if you can't adapt to where God is taking you. The children of Israel were unwilling to adapt. They refused to adapt to the cloud because they were so focused on the crowds. They couldn't adapt to the mind of empowerment because they had stayed too long in the life of disempowerment. Miracles aren't enough! God gave them the rock to drink from. Mind you that rock was Christ. (I Cor. 10:4) They experienced supernatural food and supernatural power over their clothing and shoes. They saw and felt the presence of God daily. It wasn't enough. Miracles are never enough; you have to have a change of mind to enter the land of promise, the land of TURN-AROUND!

4. **FEAR:** Fear always moves you away from faith. Fear will always paralyze movement and increase. When God finally brought the children of Israel to the borders of the Promised Land, they saw the enemy and their self-image cost them dearly. Their fear decided their self-image. They said, "We can't fight them, for we are mere grasshoppers in their sight." (Numbers 13:33)

5. **STUBBORNNESS:** Let's deal with this one later!

6. **COMPLAINING:** I believe complaining is offensive to God. No matter what God did for the children of Israel, it was never enough. They were always in need of something else. Needy people are never satisfied. Welfare minded people are never grateful. Ungratefulness is a killer to a giver. God isn't going to bless an unthankful heart.

7. **YOUR PAST:** When you are focused on where you came from, you miss the ability to see where you are going. The quickest way to stay imprisoned to your present is to hold on to your past. It's not that you can't learn from your past, but you cannot live there. This is why the rearview mirror in your car is much smaller than the windshield. You're only supposed to glance at your past, not stare at it.

8. **STRIFE:** What is strife? When you are vigorous, in bitter conflict, sow discord or antagonism with others. The children of Israel were always competing with what God said. They never accepted God or His leaders' instructions without complaint. Strife can birth bitterness. Bitterness can cause strife. When someone is still hurting over an offense, they can be very hard to instruct or train. It will eventually keep you stuck in the wilderness.

I don't know about you, but I have decided that I'm not staying here. I have decided that I'm going to end this year with more than what I began it with. I have decided that I'm going to experience my **turn-around** this year! **How about you?**

God rarely moves people toward comfort before He moves you toward promise. What is the proof you've entered the Promised Land? Opposition, giants, crisis and warfare are an indicator that you have arrived.

*"The LORD said, "I have indeed seen the misery of my people in Egypt. I have heard them crying out because of their slave drivers, and I am concerned about their suffering. So I have come down to rescue them from **the hand** of the Egyptians and to bring them up out of **that land** into a good and spacious land, a land flowing with milk and honey... And now the cry of the Israelites has reached me, and I have seen the way the Egyptians are oppressing them." Exodus 3: 7- 10*

God brought His people out of slavery. They had been in that condition for quite some time; roughly 400 years. In that length of time, a few generations were born and died. Those living were born into slavery, working for the Egyptians. None of the Israelites that came out of slavery knew Joseph or remembered the time when they were a mighty nation. All they were living on was what use to be, what might have been or what should be. When they got tired, they cried out to God for help. Isn't this really what God desires from us; to realize that there are areas in our lives that will never change if God doesn't get involved? God said to Moses, "Tell them I've seen and heard."

You are on your way out of your crisis when you have God's focus. In the next season, God will send a deliver. God also said, "I am concerned about their suffering". What a Father! He knows where we are hurting. He knows and He can bear witness to our pains. He is a God who feels what you are feeling and won't just leave you there. Help is on the way!

DELIVER THEM FROM THE HAND AND FROM THE LAND

Here's where the passage loses me! God took them out of a bad place of bondage and then He took them where? Not to some posh island or a place where they could live in peace. God took them to an occupied land full of nations that were mightier than them. To do this God uses two focal points, hand and land. There is a powerful truth here.

Hand of bondage: This represents the bondage of movement. They were bound to the power of the hand of their enemy. They were told when to get up and when to go to bed. They were commanded to work and toil, not for their own wealth but for the wealth of another. Egypt wouldn't have even been in this prosperous place if it weren't for Israel. Joseph gave them the wisdom to survive a famine that would have most likely destroyed all of Egypt. They were bound for so long that they didn't know another way of living except to be told what to do and when to do it. They were living under the hand of what someone else wanted from them.

Sounds like what is happening every day. People get up and go to work, clock in when they are told to, clock out when they are told to and go on vacation when they are told they can. Many today are living under the hand of bondage.

Taking us out of the hand isn't enough. God knows this. He can deliver you from your job… from the slavery of another. God could have come down and conquered the Egyptians and removed them from being the hand of bondage over his children. However, God knew it wouldn't be enough. It's the same reason why some people win the lottery but eventually find themselves back in the same financial status they were before they won. It doesn't matter how much money someone is given, if they do not understand the principle attached to wealth, they will find themselves back in bondage to lack and debt. You will remain enslaved to your current situation until your mind starts thinking like the season you want to be in!

Land of bondage: This is the freedom of thinking. God wanted more than to just set them free from a taskmaster. God wanted to change their mentality. If your mind doesn't change, you are done! As long as the children of Israel had the same thinking, they would have eventually gone back into bondage to another nation. God needed to free their minds. They needed to shift from a disempowered mind to an empowered mind. God had to move them from the land where they had been beat up and destroyed. He had to move them into the wilderness to prepare them for a mind cleansing. The only way to do this was to move them into a land where they would have to **confront**, **fight** and **possess**. The children of Israel had to face the enemy. An enemy is the door to your next reward. When God decides to reward you, He will schedule a conflict for you to face and fight. Think about it. When do you usually experience increase and change? It was probably after a great battle, conflict or problem.

> **Reward is Usually Hidden Behind the Door of an Enemy**

Reward is the next season after a conquered battle. Make sure you never go to war where there are no spoils. Don't exhaust yourself in a fight or crisis unless you will receive increase on the other side of victory. You don't need to go to battle unless the enemy you defeat can promote you to more. Those are the times you need to move on and forget it. Not every enemy is worth fighting.

There were many nations in the land of promise. God didn't need them to fight all of them, just the ones that were greater than they were: **mightier, stronger, larger, more, bigger, richer - are you getting the picture?**

Why did God take them to a land already occupied? He wanted to change their mindset to believe they belonged in that land. You have to believe.

You have to believe you belong. God needs to know that _you believe_ you belong where another is living. The reason that God took His people to a place that was already occupied was so that they would develop the mindset that they belonged where someone else was.

You have to develop the persuasion that someone is living in your neighborhood. Someone else is living in your house and driving your car. You have to become mentally persuaded that what one man can do, another can do!

The willingness to fight is the proof you have decided where you belong!

To belong matters. If you don't believe you belong, you will never be persuaded to confront and fight. I was sitting in my office one night and a young man handed me a battle seed. This is not uncommon in my church, but when I turned over the envelope and read what he was sowing for, I was checked in my spirit. *"I am an actor... I am a fake... I am unhappy... I am tired of feeling like I'm invisible. I am sowing this battle seed because I need happiness, joy!"*

Immediately I called him back into my office. I said, *"Son, You don't sow a seed for happiness and joy. You're unhappy for a reason. A harvest of happiness is not attached to a seed; it's connected to something else. You're unhappy for a reason!"*

I asked him why he felt unhappy. He replied, "Bishop, I was in a play in December, and I invited a few people to come and watch me. When I looked out in the crowd, not one person showed up...Bishop, what's wrong with me? I feel like I am invisible and that no one really notices me in a crowd. I feel like I am a nobody..."

I looked at him and said... "Son, first of all you don't have to sow a seed for what you're asking for. Happiness isn't a harvest; happiness is a feeling, a decision. Did something happen to you as a child? Did something happen that might have downloaded a memory of insignificance?"

He replied with tears running down his face, "Yes! Bishop, I was abused by my stepmother. One time she was beating me so bad that I thought she was going to kill me. When I called for help, I saw my father coming... thinking He was coming to my aid. To my surprise he just sat there and watched. He watched Bishop, and laughed while I was being abused. I was shocked and wounded deeply."

I quickly responded, "That's it! You picked up the sense of being invisible in that moment. You had to believe that you must have

> **Your Self-Image Can Decide Whether You Stay in the Wilderness or Experience the Grapes of Promise.**

been invisible to deal with your father who should have protected you, but didn't."

You will never change what you're unwilling to confront. As a matter of fact, confrontation is always needed for change. Nothing changes without it. You have to be willing to not only face a problem but also to confront it. You must be willing to confront whoever and whatever is keeping you from change. You must prepare for warfare! Your whole life will be a battleground. There is no way to avoid it.

Those who are unwilling to fight for their rights and for their change have developed a refugee mind set. Have you ever heard of "refugee camps"? Maybe you've seen them on the news; a group of people being protected, fed and cared for by another group of people. A refugee camp is for people who will not fight so they can take flight. In any confrontation you have only two responses: fight or flight! That's it. You will either stand up to face the enemy or you will flee from him.

The tribulation you have survived is the proof of your willingness to win.

7 ENEMIES THAT YOU MUST FIGHT...7 SPIRITS THAT MUST BE CONQUERED:

The children of Israel completed their forty-year cleansing. They wandered in the wilderness until God decided to dry up and move out all who had a grasshopper mentality. It's good to take note of the fact that how you see yourself decides if you will leave the wilderness living and experience the grapes of promise.

*"When the Lord your God brings you into the land which you go to possess, and has cast out many nations before you, the **Hittites** and the **Girgashites** and the **Amorites** and the **Canaanites** and the **Perizzites** and the **Hivites** and the **Jebusites,** seven nations greater and mightier than you, and when the Lord your God delivers them over to you, you shall conquer them and utterly destroy them. You shall make no covenant with them nor show mercy to them. Nor shall you make marriages with them. You shall not give your daughter to their son, nor take their daughter for your son. For they will turn your sons away from following Me, to serve other gods; so the anger of the Lord will be aroused against you and destroy you suddenly. But thus you shall deal with them: you shall destroy their altars, and break down their sacred pillars, and cut down their wooden images, and burn their carved images with fire." Deuteronomy 7:1-5*

Take a hard look at this. God was taking His people to a place that was already established and occupied by other nations. It was a land that had to be conquered, believed and fought for if they were going to live there; a place with enemies stronger, bigger and much more equipped for battle. Their whole way of living and surviving was about to change. If they couldn't adjust to this new way of thinking, they would disqualify to enter.

At this particular time in history, there were less than one billion people on the earth! There was plenty of prime land that no one had lived on or even seen. But God doesn't want us to live in a place of comfort. He expects us to fight. The children of Israel were an example to us that we must believe who He is and who we are in Him.

We are going to take a closer look at these seven nations to see why God wanted them utterly destroyed. Make no treaty with these nations. These nations are seven spirits we must conquer if we plan to have dominion.

7 Nations…7 Spirits…7Actions

1. The Hittites: **The Spirit of Fear**.

This is the first nation mentioned. This spirit must be conquered first or the rest will win without any effort at all. The Hittites represent the spirit of FEAR! Fear is the number one hindrance that keeps most people stuck in a life they hate. Many believe that when you walk in faith you destroy fear. The truth is that fear will always accompany faith. The proof that faith is present is that fear enters the room. You will never experience faith without fear.

> **The Proof That Faith Is Present Is That Fear Is Present.**

The greatest faith is released when we face the thing that causes us the greatest fear. Faith would have no value without the cost of fear. Fear is the price of faith. When you cash in the currency of faith, you have to spend the fear. You have to move, walk and act in your faith. This is why faith is the greatest action we have. Faith is the only thing that heaven responds to.

- God doesn't respond to needs or everyone in need would have their needs met.
- God doesn't respond to crying. He hears our cries, but doesn't respond to them.
- God doesn't respond to complaining.
- God doesn't respond to prayer unless that prayer is offered up with another ingredient: Faith.

God is moved by our faith, responds to faith, and releases favor on a faith lived life.

We have to deal with this spirit of fear. Fear causes spiritual paralyses. Fear stops the very action of faith. You have to conquer fear at every level in order to walk a life of faith. You cannot make a treaty with fear, nor marry into fear, nor give it over to your sons or daughters. Fear is the enemy to any move of God. Fear is a mental block that focuses on the problem and not the promotion. Fear has a voice. It speaks in the parts of your mind where you have doubt and worry.

Doubt and worry are the wood that keeps the fire of fear burning hot in our lives. Where there is no wood, guess what? The fire goes out! If fear is to remain, it will open the door to the next enemy: the Girgashites.

2. The Girgashites: **Looking Back... Living in the past!**

The spirit of fear births the seed to live in the past and to never allow your mind to dream for tomorrow. If you are stuck in your present life, it's because you haven't overcome the mistakes, failures and regrets of the past. The only way to leave your present and enter your future is with your mind. Your dreams and imaginations allow you to see your future, and if you can't release your dreams then you will be stuck in your present life. You will be imprisoned to your now. Your now isn't really now... it is your past being relived in your present.

There's never any advancement in your life if your focus is always on what went wrong in your past. Let's be real. We all have a past. We all have failed. We all have done stupid. There's not a person alive who doesn't wish they could go back and fix something from their past.

I was speaking in Trussville, Alabama, a few years ago. Trussville is the city where I graduated from high school. When I left that city, I was headed to Bible school. It took me thirty years to return to that city to preach. The night that I arrived, I couldn't believe how much the city had changed. I found myself in a sleepless night with all kinds of thoughts flooding my mind.

I got up the next morning and told my travel assistant to pull the truck up. I wanted to go see the places where I grew up. While I was driving down some of the roads that I had walked so many times as a teenager, I had this thought; *"What if I could go back in time and see myself walking down this road right now. The time wouldn't be 2011, but 1977. I wouldn't be a 49-year-old man, but a boy just trying to find my way. What would I say if I could pull this truck over and mentor the boy that I was by the man that I had become? What would I tell him to do, to avoid and to spend more focus on?"*

I became so sad because I began to see all the wasted time, worry and energy that had seemed so big then, but now was small and trivial. I could feel tears welling up in my eyes. I wanted to mentor that young boy so bad. I wanted to tell him to be a better student, and to let him know that life isn't about who you hang out with as much as it is about what you learn along the journey. I wanted to grab him and say, "Wake up, boy! Get ready! Life is about decisions." But I can't. I can't change any of it. The past is there and even though there's good and bad, it was necessary to form and create what I have become today. I can't let the spirit of the Girgashites live in my mind. The past keeps you anchored to your present.

3. The Amorites: **Wrong Conversation… Negative Words.**

You are living today a conversation that you had yesterday!

When the children of Israel were finally at the place to conquer and move into their next season, it wasn't this enemy as a nation that kept them from entering. It was a nation in the spirit realm. Not one conflict had happened yet. The only thing they had done so far was send 12 spies to see what the land had to offer.

The soil was rich, the land was flowing with prosperity and the vineyards were yielding grapes the size of watermelons. Everything was as the Lord promised, but they decided to talk about the enemy. They couldn't stop talking about how big the enemy was. Their conversation was squashing their promise! ***Conversation is the vehicle by which vision and faith are destroyed or built.*** Their conversation cost them dearly. They all died in the wilderness, except for Joshua and Caleb; they maintained a right conversation. Could your conversation be the very thing that's keeping you stuck? Fight this spirit; destroy it; make no treaty with it!

*"And they brought up an evil report of the land which they had searched unto the children of Israel, saying, The land, through which we have gone to search it, is a land that eateth up the inhabitants thereof; and all the people that we saw in it are men of a great stature. And there we saw the giants, the sons of Anak, which come of the giants: and we were in our own sight as **grasshoppers**, and so we were in their sight."* Numbers 13:32-33

4. The Canaanites: **Spirit of Pride, Stubbornness, Stiff necked.**

Be cautious as a believer that you don't mistake stubbornness as determination. Many in the church do this and believe they are working their faith. They think they are standing on the verse, *"When you've done all you can do just stand..."* Ephesians 6:13. Many mistake stubbornness as determination and use their will to fight God's will.

When you're planning on winning battles for God, you must give up who you are and what you want and become what God desires for you to be. All the leaders in the Bible that God used greatly gave up their will for His. No one can win the battle for Promised Land living if they are carrying their own will. These seven nations represent the seven spirits that will try to destroy us when we begin to experience Promised Land living.

Let me tell you why I believe this is the most damaging of these seven. I can observe what you're doing but I cannot tell you why you're doing it. I believe the spider that all sin begins with is the spirit of pride and stubbornness. Christians spend most of their walk attempting to keep their hearts clean from the spider web of sin, failure and disobedience. I don't believe that people want to be sinners. I don't believe that the hearts of people want to be bad; I believe they desire to be good. We have been sold a lie in religion that our works are the focus of our walk. When works are our focus, Jesus isn't. We don't have to try and "be good". We must understand that we are good in Jesus. We can't allow this mindset to remain in the Kingdom. Jesus must be exercised and used, for His ministry was the ministry of redemption, restoration and recovery. In Him we live and find ourselves. Paul said it this way:

"In Him we live, and move, and have our being… for we are his offspring." Acts 17:28

The Difference Between Stubbornness and Determination:

Determination means a *firmness of purpose, decisions on a course of actions, fixed purpose!* Some words that describe determination are willpower, resolve, fortitude, grit, strength of mind and strength of character.

Stubbornness means *unreasonably determined…hard to move.* Words that describe stubbornness are inflexibility, headstrong, and unreasonable thinking.

Stubbornness is the mindset that you know you should, but won't. It is a way that says I have a made up mind and refuse to hear truth. The Bible uses the word "stiff necked" quite a few times which means the refusal to be turned. God cannot use nor can He bless anyone who refuses to be changed, led or taught.

FACTS ABOUT STUBBORNNESS:

1. God will turn you over to your own desires. Psalms 81:11
2. Stubbornness will cause you to move backwards in life. Jeremiah 7:24
3. Stubbornness can unlock the curses of the covenant

instead of the blessings. Jeremiah 11:8
4. Stubbornness keeps you from being protected. Hosea 4:16
5. An angry spirit proves stubbornness.
6. A stubborn heart makes you useless to God and the Kingdom. Jeremiah 13:10
7. Stubbornness stores up God's wrath over your life. Romans 2:5

5. The Perizzites: **A confused mind that is always questioning God's instructions.**

What got you out, will never take you in. You must remember this when you are ready to walk in the promise. It will require a different mindset. You will never take your promise when you have a mind that is always questioning God, always wondering and trying to figure out what God is doing.

A double minded person is always unstable. James 1:8 says that when you have two thoughts or opinions you can never really make up your mind to fight. You will always flee instead of fight. It is impossible to have two mindsets and walk in faith. Faith has one mind and that is the mind of Christ. When you decide to walk in prosperity or promise, you will have to fight and defeat the Perizzites. This confused and double-minded thinking keeps you stuck in the wilderness. God doesn't give us instructions to sit around discussing and trying to figure them out. He gives them so you can open the door of promise with your faith of obedience.

6. The Hivites: **The Spirit of Complacency.**

This spirit has taken over in our churches. This is a spirit of laziness; a do nothing spirit. It's where a group of people gather to enjoy and take, but never have the fortitude to add. I hate this spirit! This spirit is revealed in the lives of those who aren't really living; they are merely existing.

Look around your church and schools; watch the actions of our youth. This spirit is growing at an alarming rate with television, Xbox 360 and all the video games on the market. Society has conditioned our nation to sit and do nothing. This attitude is now breeding over into the church. When you ask for help…when you ask for workers…the few show up and the many live in a spirit of complacency.

Monitor the leadership in our country. In case you don't know it, I'm speaking about America. Poor leadership happens when voters become complacent and won't vote for the right issues. The Hivites are living strong in our country. This is why we see very little Promised Land dwellers in our churches.

7. The Jebusites: **False Witness, Gossip, Destroying the Character of Another.**

I believe that out of all of these spirits this one offends God the most. Demons don't destroy ministries; people do. They do it through false witness, gossip and rumors. Many people have said so much wrong about me and my ministry over the past 30 years. They do this to justify their bad decisions. There is no 'promised living' with the person who loves to talk and spread gossip about another person.

This is such a cancerous spirit. Why does it happen? Most people compete with others because they are damaged in their own identity and calling. They spend most of their lives wishing to have what someone else has and they can never discover their own purpose and calling. Anger is birthed when they can't have what others have. What does that angry person do? They start to compete, and what happens when we compete? We have to win. What happens when you can't win because it isn't your game? You spread false witness about those you've competed with.

Warfare is your destiny. Warfare is my destiny. Our warfare isn't against people, and in my opinion, it really isn't the devil either. The warfare you will fight daily is in your own mind!

CHAPTER FIVE

ORDER NEVER
HAPPENS RANDOMLY

*"In the beginning God created the heavens and the
earth. The earth was without form, and void; and
darkness was on the face of the deep. And the Spirit of
God was hovering over the face of the waters. Then God
said, "Let there be light"; and there was light."*
Genesis 1:1-3

*7*o take you further into this truth that we just studied in the previous chapter, we must journey back to the beginning and see what really happened and what is really taking place. Hidden in the book of Genesis is not only an account of creation but also the power of God's purpose. God didn't just create a universe, but a system for man to walk in the image of God on the earth.

"So God created human beings in his own image in the image of God he created them; male and female he created them." Genesis 1:27 NLT

There should be something about us that looks and acts like our Creator. We were created to do something. We were not created to work for a living. We were not created to compete with one another, hate one another or be jealous of what others have. When we exemplify these traits, we reveal that we are still living according to the fallen state of man and not the position we were created for.

IN THE BEGINNING

First, we must remember that in the beginning the earth was dark, formless and empty. The earth was in utter chaos. God was attracted to the earth; thus God is attracted to chaos. There is something about chaos that draws God's focus. What good is it to be God and have no one or nothing to show Your powers to? God is attracted to chaos because chaos is where He can exercise His power to create. God created the heavens and the earth but left it in an empty, dark and formless state so that when He entered into it, He could speak to it and tell it what to become. This is what God expects us to do when we see chaos. God is attracted to chaos but He hovers over the face of the deep.

Have you ever heard of a word called "Entropy?" This word is written in the earth's default code. The word simply means, "anything left to itself will bend toward chaos." Nothing left on its own will ever move toward order. It will always move in the law of entropy toward chaos and deteriorate. I've heard that a house will deteriorate faster when it's uninhabited because there isn't someone in that house stopping the law of entropy. A yard left unattended will never grow grass but will always grow weeds. I can't tell you how much money and effort I have spent on my yard. Every year my yard seems to grow weeds more than grass. I have to fertilize it, lime it, aerate and over seed it every year. I have to get involved in order to maintain a healthy lawn. It requires a higher level of being to call order to chaos.

Order doesn't just happen randomly

Let's silence the evolutionist here. It is impossible for a one-cell animal to become tired of being one cell, start swimming, get tired of swimming, start crawling, become tired of crawling and rise up to walk. I know this to be true because God has built chaos into the universe. So when we see ORDER we immediately know that it just didn't happen. Order doesn't occur randomly.

Order means a greater force has been exercised over chaos. When we see order, we should start looking for the source that is greater than chaos, which is calling order to a disordered and chaotic world.

It is here where we see the power of God at work. I am an **ordered being**; something greater than me must exist because I couldn't have created or designed who I am. I began a quest for this source of the force that has called order to a chaotic universe. I realize that I can't praise the beast of the field because man is created higher than the beasts of the fields. I must look beyond myself to a higher being in my quest for understanding.

I realize I can't look at creation because I am made higher than creation. I can't look at angels because I am created higher than the angels. When I look up to see what is higher than man, I realize that the only being higher than me is God. So my focus, my praise, my worship and my giving is all to Him. The force of the source that has called order to my chaos is God. Man is created a little lower than God. We are His handiwork.

"LORD, our Lord, how majestic is your name in all the earth! You have set your glory in the heavens. Through the praise of children and infants you have established a stronghold against your enemies, to silence the foe and the avenger. When I consider your heavens, the work of your fingers, the moon and the stars, which you have set in place, what is mankind that you are mindful of them, human beings that you care for them? You have made them a little lower than the angels and crowned them with glory and honor. You made them rulers over the works of your hands; you put everything under their feet: all flocks and herds, and the animals of the wild, the birds in the sky, and the fish in the sea, all that swim the paths of the seas..." Psalms 8: 1-8

CHAOS IS THE DEFAULT POSITION.

Wherever there is chaos, force has not been exercised over it.

Since chaos is built into the system, wherever there is chaos someone has defaulted their position. Someone has failed to exercise order over chaos.

If our schools are in chaos, then our teachers are out of the position of exercising a force that is greater than the chaos. When there is chaos in our government, our churches or our families, someone is out of position. We know this because we know order doesn't just happen randomly! We are made in God's image and likeness. When the world around us is formless, void and dark, the only way to fix it is for someone to speak to it and tell it what to be! *"God said... Let there be... and it was!"*

GOD SETS MAN IN THE PLACE OF ORDER AND PLANTS A GARDEN.

What happened in the garden? God would appear and speak to man. God only speaks in the place of order. What was the first thing He commanded man when God spoke?

*"...God said unto them, **Be fruitful**, and **multiply**, and **replenish the earth**, and **subdue it**: and **have dominion over** the fish of the sea, and over the fowl of the air, and over every living thing that moveth upon the earth."* Genesis 1:28

Pay close attention to the sequence of God's order. They are contingent to one another. To get out of sequence will create chaos.

1. *Be fruitful*
2. *Multiply*
3. *Replenish the earth*
4. *Subdue it*
5. *Then have dominion over it*

Sequence Matters!

God is a God of order. He is a God of sequence. Order is simply doing what is supposed to be done first. Order is the accurate arrangement of things. God is obsessed with order. His principles create order. When we walk and exercise order in our lives, comfort will be produced. God moves in the order of progress. When you are taking inventory of your life, notice how sequence matters to almost everything you do. You wake up before you get up.

Order Creates Comfort

Routine is the best way to create order. The same two keys for failure are the same two keys for success:

- Habit
- Routine

A habit is what I am addicted to. Routine creates my habits. What I am doing daily is deciding what I am becoming permanently. When I change my habits, I eventually affect my routine. When I change my routine, then I am changed.

We must move in sequence. It's very important to follow God's pattern. We should focus first on being **fruitful** before attempting to multiply. Many are trying to work the prosperity message before they understand the Gospel message. The problem is that this is exactly what the world does. It's called self-ambition. Ambition is how Nimrod attempted to succeed without the power and favor of God. The danger of multiplying before being fruitful is that the unfruitfulness will multiply or increase.

Take a look around. Many "Christians" are living an **unfruitful** life. I'm not speaking about materialism (*money, cars, and stuff*). The fruit that God notices is spiritual fruit, or spiritual maturity. Whatever happened to passion for sharing our faith and bringing people to church? Where did our passion for Jesus go? It looks like we've replaced it with the prosperity of Heaven. We need to work and focus on both; to be a good witness we need to be prosperous. Don't forsake one for the other. Work both laws!

Subdue, and then have dominion.

God said to subdue the earth and then to have dominion over the beast. There is a difference between subdue and dominion. There is an order and that order is to be fruitful, multiply, replenish the earth and **subdue** the earth.

- Subdue: The word subdue is defined as "to bring somebody under forcible control." It means to "soften something, to repress emotions." Subdue has a very powerful authority behind it. When we decide to do something about our chaos, it will take the power to subdue to change it.
- Dominion: Dominion means "to have territorial control," not just control but the power of ruler-ship over that

territory. Dominion means "to be self-governing...a sphere of influence...power!"

It is possible to subdue but never take control of your territory. When we subdue, we've decided to lean into chaos and command order to it. Remember, chaos is the default on the earth. So when you see chaos, you should immediately realize that someone failed to subdue or exercise order over it. Subdue is when you decide not to get into agreement to your chaos but instead to lean into it. Use the force and strength of your faith to speak to the chaos. Tell it what you want it to become. Do not get into agreement with your chaos; subdue it, form it, create through it. When you are facing a mountain that is too large to climb and too wide to walk around, then do what Jesus anointed us to do. **Speak to it!** Tell it where to go, to be removed from your pathway (Mark 11:23).

When I began to learn the sequence of this order and to walk in it, I gained control and power over my land and territory. Be fruitful, multiply, subdue then have dominion. Unfortunately, many in our churches are attempting to walk in dominion before they subdue, before they multiply and before they reproduce any fruit. The reason for power is because you have multiplied. The need for more is because you have increased your level of influence. You have no need for power and order if you are never attempting to be more, have more or want more. Let me interject here; your wants have to be bigger than materialistic focus. Your desire for more can't be because you are in competition with someone else. You can't desire more just because you want a new car or house. Those things matter and God wants us to have our desires, but things can't be the primary purpose for subduing and desiring dominion. The focus to your increase has to be....

> **Dominion is Only Granted Because You've Chosen to Multiply!**

1. God's purpose.
2. God's interest.
3. Others who have less than you do.
4. Then, you!

I heard someone ask, *"Do you want joy?"* Then put **Jesus** first, **others** second and **you** last. Do you notice the acronym?

Subduing is a redirecting of my faith and the resources around me *to lean into chaos and bring it, by force, into order!* That force is your faith spoken through your mouth into the formless, empty, dark places of your life. We must now move to the voice. Without voice and the power of God's voice behind ours, we will have no power at all. All we are going to do is make a lot of religious noise. **Noise is meaningless sound.**

The Danger of Second Voices

When you have two voices speaking to you, your mind begins to enter into the question mode. When your mind starts to question voices, it starts to break down in its own power of commitment and decision. Confusion is the proof that someone has questioned your last decision and instruction. In God's presence there can only be one voice speaking and that voice is His. When we allow someone else to speak to us, we begin to weaken our own resolve and commitments. The other voice doesn't weaken God's voice, but it weakens your ability to receive and stay connected to it. This happens because you've allowed something to enter into your mind that wasn't sent by God.

God's Power is Attached to His Voice

*"Now the serpent was **craftier** than any of the wild animals the LORD God had made. **He said** to the woman, **"Did God really say, 'You must not eat from any tree in the garden?'"**....Then the man and his wife **heard the sound of the Lord God** as he was walking in the garden in the cool of the day, and they hid from the Lord God among the trees of the garden. But the Lord God called*

to the man, *"Where are you?"* He answered, *"I heard you in the garden, and I was afraid because I was naked; so I hid."* And he said, *"Who told you that you were naked? Have you eaten from the tree that I commanded you not to eat from?"* Genesis 3:1, 8-11

Did you notice the bold-typed phrases in the verses above? Let's break down the power of this so we can start reconnecting to the right voice.

Craftier: This word describes Satan. He is clever, crafty and smooth at twisting what God has said. The enemy's plan is to destroy what God's word was sent to do. The enemy doesn't say God is wrong nor does he attack God! The enemy attacks what God has said by adding questions to the instruction. When the second voice starts questioning your first decision it will create confusion, Confusion is the proof an enemy has entered your environment. Think about the times in your life when you have experienced confusion. When your relationships begin to break down, it is because you have started to question the other person's voice, words and actions. That second voice in your mind causes you to begin judging, criticizing and becoming confused with the relationship. Then you start breaking down in your ability to communicate and hear effectively.

> **The Tribulation You've Survived is the Proof of Your Willingness to Succeed**

Now, the first voice becomes nothing but noise. Noise is meaningless sound. This is Satan's greatest tactic. This is his greatest and most clever work; not to disprove God, not to attack God but to attack His words. His instructions! All the blessings of protection and increase are attached to His words. *"The serpent was more cunning and he deceived mankind. Did God really say...?"*

"Heard the sound of The Lord..." Now Adam and Eve became confused. They didn't even recognize the entry of the Lord. All they could hear was a loud sound and meaningless noise.

They didn't have the power to recognize because they didn't have the voice of understanding. When they lost their connection to the voice of God, they lost their power to put order into their chaos. When I lose my connection to the place of the voice, I lose my **power** to deal with chaos. They lost the fruit of their hearing. You must understand the power of hearing.

- *The fruit of hearing increases my faith.*
- *The fruit of faith increases my order.*
- *The fruit of order decides and creates how the blessings come.*

When I lose my hearing, I lose my understanding. I end up lost in my crisis. When I lose my connection to the place of the voice, I lose my power to deal with the source of chaos and become disconnected from the blessing. The power of God isn't in His presence **but in His voice**. His words have the power to put order into our chaos. We spend most of our time in church seeking God's presence more that seeking His Word. We have catered to the ear of emotion and comfort instead of the ear to hear. Those who have an ear let them hear. Hearing happens when we understand what we hear. When we hear, but lack understanding, our mind interprets that as sound or noise and then breaks down into a confused state. We must hear with understanding! They shall know the truth, and the truth they know will set them free. (John 8:32)

"Where are you?" You and I both know that God did not lose Adam. How can a God who knows everything lose the only people in His Garden? He didn't! God was asking Adam where he had gone. God knew where Adam was, but did Adam know where he was? Did he understand what he had done and where he had fallen? Did he know that his decision had cost him the only source that could redeem him?

You must know where you've been if you want to decide where you are going.

This was the real question God was asking, *"Adam, do you even know where you are?"* If you can't tell me where you are, where you have fallen or where you've been, you will never be able to decide where you're going from here. Your present is stuck to your past. Your present is now permanent. This may not seem like much but this is very important. I lived through the "name it and claim it" era where people were taught not to let anyone know what they were going through. Maybe you've experienced this kind of teaching; afraid to tell anyone what you are feeling or facing because you don't want to have a "bad confession."

How can you unlock the healing power of Jesus if you can't confess that you're sick? When I confess I'm sick, I can unlock my healing! If I confess I'm broke, then Jesus becomes my prosperity!

We have been given wrong teachings. It is only through tribulations that God can reveal His value and power. The tribulation you've survived is the proof of your willingness to succeed! We have to come back to right theology. We have to get back to Biblical teaching and not what we've been taught from denomination.

*"These people honor me with their lips, but their hearts are far from me. They worship me in vain; their **teachings are merely human rules**." Matthew 15: 8,9*

*"You have a fine way of setting aside the commands of God in order **to observe your own traditions**!... Thus **you nullify the word of God by your tradition** that you have handed down. And you do many things like that." Mark 7:9,13*

*"See to it that no one takes you **captive through hollow and deceptive philosophy,** which depends **on human tradition** and the basic principles of this world rather than on Christ." Colossians 2:8*

We can't train people in the church the way we should for several reasons. First, they won't stay committed to training and correction. Second, new people come with bad training and wrong denominational baggage. When you try to show them where the error is and what is needed for change they fight you. They fight the truth because of their traditions. We won't see where we've been and where we are so that we can ignite the desire and inspiration to change.

Too many charismatic churches want to be entertained instead of trained. The majority of them swarm from conference to conference. They've become '**Conference Groupies**;' blessing seekers who only want to have a "good time." Faddish and fickle, they are like the 'loaves and fishes' crowd that followed Jesus to see the miracles (Mark 6:52). These folks will walk away the moment they are challenged with the high calling to eat of His flesh and to drink of His blood. They will unplug as soon as you challenge them to change and get involved. These Christians want heaven, but they have no desire to promote or build the Kingdom! If we don't call order to the body of Christ, we are going to miss the greatest time in the church age. This is the time for the Bridegroom to appear and take His Bride, the church, back to where He is.

GOD WILL NOT SPEAK UNTIL HE SEES ORDER!

The pattern in Genesis teaches us that chaos drew God, but it was not chaos that the Spirit dwelt over.

*"Now the earth was formless and empty, darkness was over the surface of the deep, and the **Spirit of God was hovering over the waters**."Genesis 1:2*

I was curious as to why the Spirit wanted to hang out over the water. I noticed it wasn't the water that drew God, but it was the chaos. One evening my wife and I were enjoying a night on the lake. The water was so calm and still that the lake appeared to be one large mirror. It looked like a solid, clear floor of glass. I was standing in the rear of the boat looking at the sunset and the crystal-like glass lake. Looking over the bow into the water, I could see the reflection of the sky and myself so clearly. It was so vivid that I started to lose my depth perception and clarity to which side was real.

That evening it dawned on me. God's Spirit wanted to hover over the water because He could see His image. He was drawn by the confusion of chaos, but it was His image that kept God there.

God spoke when He saw Himself in the water. The Bible says we are made in His image and likeness. God will speak order into our chaos when He sees His image in us.

This is what we see in the story of creation in Genesis. God spoke light into existence on the first day.

"And God said, 'Let there be light,' and there was light. God saw that the light was good, and he separated the light from the darkness. God called the light 'day,' and the darkness he called 'night.' And there was evening, and there was morning—the first day." Genesis 1:3-5

It is interesting that God spoke light on the second day, but on the fourth day He created and named sources of light. One light is greater than the other light.

"God made two great lights—the greater light to govern the day and the lesser light to govern the night. He also made the stars." Genesis 1:16

These two lights are the sun and the moon, and the sun is the greater light that shines in the day. The moon is the lesser light because it can't shine without reflecting the sun. This is a type and shadow of what was to come. Jesus died on the cross, resurrected from the grave and is now sitting at the right hand of the Father. Jesus is the light that shines from the power that is within Him. We are the moons of the darkness. We have the ability to be a light in the darkness when we are in the right position to reflect the son!

God speaks to man's spirit when He sees Himself. When you reflect Jesus, God will give you the power to call order into chaos. We see this example in the baptism of Jesus (Matthew 3:13-17). God saw His reflection once again in the water when Jesus was baptized in the Jordan. God opened the heavens and declared, *"This is my beloved Son in whom I am well pleased."* The reflection of Jesus looking through the water gave God the voice to speak.

Once you understand this, you will spend more time in the waters of His Word so you can position yourself to fully reflect the Son. You will hear the voice of God speak to you under open heavens. You must position yourself for reflection if you desire to rule in your dark times and crisis.

INSIDE OUT, UPSIDE DOWN

The miracle of childbirth gives us insight to the process of birthing our promise. Babies are born head first and feet last. The newborn has to turn inside out and upside down. This is how the church was birthed through the Son of God. God had to become man so that man could be connected to God again. The Son of God became the Son of Man, so that we can be the Sons of God.

- *We are the generation of His power.*
- *We are the generation of His workers.*
- *We are the feet of His body.*
- *We are to carry out his burden of the Gospel.*
- *We are the generation of that power that all things are now under our feet.*

Be still and restful. Go sit in the upper room. Find a place of order. Sit in God's presence. Jesus is preparing something new for us. I have a word for you today. God is doing a new thing in you, and it will be born.

Declare this right now. Do it and see what power will enter you!

> *I will do a new thing; in me it shall be born. I will do a new thing, His wonders to perform. Now I reach my healing hand to bring my word to you. Remember not the things of old, for a new thing I will do. He's making all things new; He's making all new things!* **He's making all things new!**

CHAPTER SIX

CHECK YOURSELF BEFORE YOU WRECK YOURSELF!

Attitudes are generally positive or negative views of a person, place, thing or event.

"I can't change the direction of the wind, but I can adjust my sails to always reach my destination." James Dean

"Our attitudes toward life determine life's attitude towards us." John N. Mitchell

*$\mathcal{A}$ttitudes are judgments. They develop on the **ABC** model (affect, behavior and cognition). The affective response is an emotional response that expresses an individual's degree of preference for an entity. The behavioral intention is a verbal indication or typical behavioral tendency of an individual. The cognitive response is a cognitive evaluation of the entity that constitutes an individual's beliefs about the object. Most attitudes are the result of either direct experience or observational learning from the environment.[v]*

The first time I heard the phrase, "check yourself before you wreck yourself," I thought it was crazy. When I began to meditate on those words it made deeper sense. We would probably live an easier life if we would stop long enough to check our feelings before we react to them.

The first thing we need to check is our attitude. Our attitude needs to be addressed and monitored every single day. Attitude has to be one of our main focuses. Your attitude should reflect your best ideas and feelings, not your problems.

INNER ATTITUDE

Most people are good at faking a positive attitude. We have learned how to act the way we want to be perceived by others. We see the boss coming and start talking the way we perceive the boss wants us to talk. Though this works for a time, it will not move God's favor toward your life. The ***healed*** life is a life that has to focus on the inner person. When the inner person is healed and intact, the outer person will always have the right attitude. How you respond to negative people and negative situations are clues to how strong your inner man is.

Law of Center

What is happening in you is deciding what is happening around you. It doesn't matter how well rounded the wheel is, if the axle isn't placed in the center of that wheel, it is useless. The same is true with your life. This is the law of center. If your center is off, your life can become useless. The axle of your life has to be in the center of your life.

5 Keys to a Powerful Center

1) Make God your first priority. Confess God's son, Jesus, as your King.
2) Make the Word of God important. You will never grow to a better you if you don't study the Word of God. Don't just read it; allow it to read you.
3) Decide to love everyone. Hell has no weapon against a person who decides to walk in love. Love is a powerful weapon and tool for a good center. Love covers others. Love is more powerful than anyone is telling you. Love is not a defense to attack but a weapon that destroys attack. If they can't change your feelings, they can't change you.
4) Don't compete with others. The biggest mistake you will make in life is to compete with another person. First, the earth will never run out of what you require to be prosperous. Second, no human on the earth has what you really need. Third, God is your source. He has an unlimited supply. Instead of looking at others and wishing that you had what they have, recognize that you have the power of Christ to work through your mind and create what you desire.
5) Take control of your own mind. Your mind is where your attitude lives. Your feelings can send wrong information to the mind and the mind can send wrong responses to your feelings. Make sure that you don't decide reactions based on what your feelings say. Have your mind to boss your feelings and not your feelings to boss your mind.

Decide to work on your inner person today. Read books, go to conferences and gather the necessary information to change your focus. This will begin to change your attitude.

What is happening around you is a clue to what is going on in you.

We all have problems. Problems and crisis almost always reveal your inner attitude.

ATTITUDE IS A CHOICE

More prayer is not the key to changing your attitude. Prayer, or mediation, does help calm the mind and purge the inner man. However, the truth is that God alone won't change your attitude. You must involve the mind. You must decide that no matter what, you are going to have a better outlook on things and on life.

I understand firsthand, through my own past mistakes and failures, how easy it is to become cynical and critical. No one, not even the greatest of people, can maintain and walk in a positive attitude with a mind that is critical and cynical over life.

THE ATMOSPHERE OF THE PALACE IS NOT DECIDED BY THE KING, BUT BY THE ATTITUDE OF THE SERVANTS.

You will never be promoted with a bad attitude. Attitude is a force that fuels your focus. Your attitude is determined by the mood you have chosen to focus on.

Attitude - *"The position or posture assumed by the body in connection with an action, feeling, mood; a manner of acting, feeling, or thinking that shows one's disposition, opinion, mental set, etc."[vi]*

- Attitude reveals your posture.

- Attitude is your behavior when things aren't going your way.
- Attitude is a window to the world of greatness.
- Your attitude creates a healthy mindset.

There is nothing you cannot be and nothing you cannot do. There is nothing you cannot have! Once you learn the simple principles of mastering a **positive attitude**, all that you want you can have. Your attitude is the key to a life of favor and connection.

Attitude can be decided through childhood. Many of us have had some sort of imprinting or pattern from our past that has formed and shaped the way we think and act. Many of the things that we do, we learned before we were ten years old. Children learn how to use their attitude to get what they want. These attitudes will become personality traits if this is not corrected.

Your attitude is the force in your life that determines whether you decrease, multiply, grow or die.

Your attitude can be an effective weapon. This is very important because all leaders and achievers are going to attract enemies. Your attitude is the physical and mental posture that your body sets up to show how it is feeling. Your attitude can cause the enemy that is attacking you to back up. Your attitude can fool the attacker into believing that the barrage of their attacks is not affecting you.

Your posture can promote a bad or good attitude. A good friend of mine gave me some great advice the other day. It was advice given to him by a very wealthy man. What others see and hear you say determines what they believe about you. When you are going through an attack or loss, make sure your body and your words are not giving you away. Look and sound like a winner even in the face of loss. This is what your attitude is. It is the power to believe even when you are suffering.

What you magnify in your mind is controlling your attitude.

To build your life, your relationships, your family and even your business, it will require a positive mind and a good attitude towards your future.

You will experience a lot of different people throughout your lifetime. Build on your strengths and never allow what others do to determine how you are going to act. Never allow others to decide how you're going to feel. Never let what is happening around you to decide your attitude. Keep your focus and your attitude on high at all times. Your attitude will allow you the necessary elevation to see above your problem and into the season of your promotion.

CHAPTER SEVEN

"HONOR!"
GUARANTEED LAW FOR RECOVERY

*"He has **honor** if he holds himself to an ideal of conduct though it is inconvenient, unprofitable, or dangerous to do so." Walter Lippmann*

"The most tragic thing in the world is a man of genius who is not a man of honor." George Bernard Shaw

I can tell your future by those you've chosen to honor.

I was sitting in a conference a few years ago listening to Dr. Mike Brown, a powerful and anointed man of God, teach on the seeds of honor. I had never thought about the word honor until I heard this message from <u>Dr. Brown.</u>

"...But now the Lord declare; Far be it from Me for those who honor Me I will honor, and those who despise Me shall be lightly esteemed." 1 Samuel 2:30 NASB

One of the most overlooked laws in the Bible is the Law of Honor, especially in the twenty-first century. Just watch the news. Observe the attitude of young people and you will see that we are raising up a generation who lack honor. Honor is a master key for promotion and protection.

I once saw a documentary about Donald Trump. The interviewer was asked what one of Mr. Trump's greatest qualities was. He said that Mr. Trump was kind to everyone and honored people. Robert Kiyosaki said that he once used the phrase "little people" in one of their television shows. Mr. Kiyosaki said that Donald Trump stopped the show and said, *"I don't like that phrase, 'little people'. There are no little people. All of us have greatness in us."* This is the proof of honor. I was impressed to watch these two wealthy men teaching kindness and respect for others.

We have become a people of dishonor, not only in the secular world, but also in our churches. Contrary to popular belief, the Man of God is one of the most important people in our lives.

- ***The Man of God is our golden connection to the things of God.***
- ***The Man of God creates spiritual awareness that helps us to understand and move into the realm of the Spirit.***

- *The Man of God is a door to our next season.*
- *The Man of God will lead us into the promise.*

One of the greatest decisions you can make today is to show honor to those whom it is due. You may be thinking, "*I have no problem showing honor to our leaders, such as the mayor, or the president, or even men who are wealthy.*" Have you ever thought about your pastor? In my opinion, he's even greater than the men who hold government offices.

How many times have you ignored the needs of your pastor? Make a powerful decision to honor those whom God has placed in your life to lead you, pray for you and to encourage you. I could not imagine life without having someone to call "Man of God" over my life.

Honor is the seed to secure the palace for you. When you learn how to show honor, you will begin to open doors of access. It doesn't take much skill to get in the palace, but it will require great skill to maintain your position there.

Dishonor will remove you from a position to be noticed. Could all sin be traced back to the lack of honor? What you gain through intelligence, you can lose through dishonor! Every person in church can be exposed through dishonor.

Dishonor can cause seasons of pain, discomfort and loss. I believe God's focus was honor even before love and obedience. As a matter of fact, you can't love or be obedient if you can't honor. God doesn't want our love if we can't offer up our honor. We must understand that respect doesn't necessarily mean you honor someone. Satan respects God, but he will not honor Him. You will never obey what you fail to honor. The difference in people is whom they have chosen to honor.

- *Honor comes before obedience.*
- *Honor precedes favor.*
- *Honor protects favor.*
- *Honor promotes favor.*

I pastor a church and I can tell you that most people do not know how to honor those whom God has placed over them. When people leave the church without even telling the pastor why, that is dishonor. Listening to others complain about the Man of God is dishonor. Questioning the pastor's integrity and gossiping about them is dishonor. Talking about the president of our country in a demeaning way is dishonoring. Talking behind someone's back about them is also a spirit of dishonor.

Allowing others to be disrespectful about your pastor is dishonor. I really have a problem with those who say they are connected to me or my church but do not defend the church or me in my absence. It says a lot to me about a person's character and integrity when they sit silently and allow others to destroy a Man of God's reputation and influence.

I was sitting at the table with my mentor, Dr. Mike Murdock, after one of the sessions at the Wisdom Center. He said something that really impacted me from deep within. His comment was this, *"If I hadn't read the scripture that states that Wisdom is the principle thing, I would have taken up the cause for honor. I would have made honor the principle thing."*

Wow! I thought that was pretty strong. It really made me consider how much honor I haven't shown to those who have earned it.

Honor greatness and you will receive the harvest of greatness. Honor is the recognition of difference.

"Give a bonus to leaders who do a good job, especially the ones who work hard at preaching and teaching. Scripture tells us, 'Don't muzzle a working ox,' and, 'A worker deserves his pay.' Don't listen to a complaint against a leader that isn't backed up by two or three responsible witnesses." 1 Timothy 5:17-19 MSG

- *Wisdom discerns who should be honored.*
- *Favor is attached to honor.*
- *Protection is connected to honor.*

- *Dishonor is the womb where every other sin is birthed.*
- *Every act of honor adds value and increase to your life.*

TWO KINDS OF PEOPLE

I believe this valuable gift of honor will open incredible doors of favor and access. In 2 Kings chapter four we read about two kinds of women. First, the Bible speaks of a *certain* woman. This woman had lost her husband and as a result found herself in a sea of debt. Creditors were knocking on her door for payment. Her husband was one of the prophets who sat under the man of God and he had died. He left her broke and abandoned. The creditors were coming to take away her sons as payment for the father's debt.

When this widow saw the Man of God, her first reaction was to extract what had been placed within him. This is not wrong; it's just that the Bible calls her *certain*. I believe the reason the Bible calls her *certain* is that the normal and natural tendency of people is to find out what they can get from the Man of God instead of giving to him.

The first reaction is always to draw from the well; to pull until there is nothing left. It's the "all about me" attitude. It never crosses the mind of the average person to supply the Man of God's needs. I know because I've been guilty of this mentality of always pulling... always drawing... always demanding time and energy. I know ministers right now who have lost their marriages, their children and some have even departed from the faith because they were surrounded by these kinds of people. *Certain, average* and *unconcerned* people make withdrawals, but never make deposits. As a result, men and women of God become bankrupt in their heart and emotions.

GREATNESS IS THE ABILITY TO SERVE

In the last part of 2 Kings chapter four, the Bible speaks about a *great* woman. What was the difference between the *certain* woman and the *great* woman? Honor made the difference.

*"And it fell on a day, that Elisha passed to Shunem, where was a **great** woman; ...And she said unto her husband, Behold now, I **perceive** that this is an holy man of God, which passeth by us continually. Let us make a little chamber, I pray thee, on the wall; and let us set for him there a bed, and a table, and a stool, and a candlestick: and it shall be, when he cometh to us, that he shall turn in thither."* 2 Kings 4:8-10 KJV

This **great** woman had a completely different reaction to the Man of God than the **certain** woman. She saw the Man of God and immediately she said, *"I perceive this is an holy man of God, Let's build... let's make... let's do for him."* She began to create an atmosphere for this Man of God.

She created him an environment where he could...

1. Rest from his weary day.
2. Find refuge and solace for prayer.
3. Replenish his anointing.
4. Have privacy and intimacy with God....she gave him his own room.
5. Be preferred and positioned in the high place within her home.

This provided him with the necessary atmosphere that allowed for his rest. Afterwards he inquired as to what she might need from his anointing. Her life was never the same again. She sowed her seed of honor until honor was the harvest she received from the Man of God. When we begin to be a burden-lifter for those over us, God begins to lift the burden from off of our shoulders.

THREE AREAS OF HONOR

First, we must honor the Lord Most High. Failing to honor God is a huge mistake that may cost you everything. It is not a wise decision to live life void of respect and honor for God. We show honor by giving. When we withhold our tithe, we are letting God know that we do not honor Him.

As a matter of fact, God Himself told us this in the book of Malachi.

"Isn't it true that a son honors his father and a worker his master? So if I'm your Father, where's the honor? If I'm your Master, where's the respect?" God-of-the-Angel-Armies is calling you on the carpet: "You priests despise me! You say, 'Not so! How do we despise you?" Malachi 1:6 MSG

How was God dishonored? We will read more in Malachi:

"Begin by being honest. Do honest people rob God? But you rob me day after day." You ask, 'How have we robbed you?' "The tithe and the offering — that's how! And now you're under a curse — the whole lot of you — because you're robbing me. Bring your full tithe to the Temple treasury so there will be ample provisions in my Temple. Test me in this and see if I don't open up heaven itself to you and pour out blessings beyond your wildest dreams. For my part, I will defend you against marauders, protect your wheat fields and vegetable gardens against plunderers." The Message of God-of-the-Angel-Armies. "You'll be voted 'Happiest Nation.' You'll experience what it's like to be a country of grace." God-of-the-Angel-Armies says so. Malachi 3:8 -12 MSG

Second, we must honor our parents *(Exodus 20:12)*. This doesn't mean that your parents can walk all over you, especially when you are an adult. But no matter what you've been through, honor them. Don't live another day with bitterness towards your parents.

Third, we must honor those whom God has placed over us; THE MAN OF GOD!

I believe one of the major reasons we are experiencing problems and such disarray is because of the lack of honor within our churches. Have you left a church? Were you sent, or did you just *"went"*? Most aren't *sent;* they just *went* somewhere else.

Went has no authority. *Went* has no power. *Went* people can't grow any further until they go back and allow the headship to release them and *send* them properly.

What is your first reaction and what are your feelings when someone mentions a church that you once attended? Is it anger, bitterness, jealousy or resentment? Do you find yourself talking against them? If so, you left wrongly. Please listen to me; you are living under a cursed season. Stop the insanity! Go and fix this mess right now!

Life Principle: "Something you need is usually hidden in something you can't stand or dislike."

God usually hides His best in flawed vessels. If you can't stop long enough to notice this, you will leave where you are. Your life is going to become a life of unrest. You will never find where you belong. Every time the preacher begins to preach the truth about where you are at, you will get offended and do what you've always done...leave!

Listen to me; don't hate me! Trust me. You are going to be better if you will just stop and listen. God is trying to get your attention. He's trying to show you that without the Set-Man in your life, you are going to stay on a roller coaster of emotions, lack and restlessness. You are never going to find any peace.

If you can't be corrected, God will never connect you to your future.

"If the foundations are destroyed, what can the righteous do?"
Psalms 11:3 NKJV

A good friend of mine showed me this passage. It really helped me to pull my church out of some terrible disorder. I didn't understand church government and order in the early years of my church, and I did my people a grievous injustice by not teaching how to honor and respect the office and position of the MAN OF GOD.

How is the Man of God going to take his city for the King and the Kingdom if people always oppose him? What can the righteous do when they lay the foundation but then people leave and break it up? The leader has to keep rebuilding the foundation. Foundations are destroyed when people leave churches talking bad about them. They don't think they are doing evil, but they are being used by Satan to destroy foundations.

CHAPTER EIGHT

"PERSISTENCY"
THE POWER TO SURVIVE

*"Nothing in this world can take the place of **persistence**. Talent will not; nothing is more common than unsuccessful people with talent. Genius will not; unrewarded genius is almost a proverb. Education will not; the world is full of educated derelicts. **Persistence** and **determination** alone are omnipotent. The slogan "press on" has solved and always will solve the problems of the human race." Calvin Coolidge*

You haven't seen what my God can do for those who wait on Him!

I believe that this is one of the most valuable keys you will need to design your life. Wherever men and women have accumulated great wealth, you can be sure that they first acquired great persistency and endurance.

Persistency is the foundation, the cement that makes faith work. Persistency is the twin brother to excellence. One is a matter of quality; the other is a matter of time. Persistence is revealed in stubborn and enduring continuance.

Persistent is defined as the *refusing to relent; continuing in the face of opposition, interference, etc.; stubborn; persevering. Lasting without change; remaining attached permanently or for a longer than normal time; as some leave you are still connected; remaining essentially unchanged.*

Success Grows On the Tree of Persistency

It's the persistency of water that causes the hard surface of the mountain to give in. The rocks are stronger than the water, but over time the persistency of the water begins to persuade the rocks to give in and conform to its will.

LAW OF EVENTUALITY

When one does something long enough, he will eventually win. Keep swinging the axe and the tree will fall no matter how big it is.

Without persistency you will be defeated before you even get started. However, with a persistent mind you will eventually win. I promise you the rewards are great for the person who can persevere and persist until the universe gives up its secrets for success.

"And let us not get tired of doing what is right, for after a while we will reap a harvest of blessing if we don't get discouraged and give up. That's why whenever we can we should always be kind to everyone, and especially to our Christian brothers." Galatians 6:9-10 TLB

There is no substitute for the master key of persistence. You can't move forward without it. You will never experience a full and satisfied life without the consciousness of persistency. Persistency is your insurance policy to success. When you're feeling the burden of your endeavor and the rewards for your efforts are taking longer than first expected, persistency will break the wall of failure and move you into the realm of success and freedom.

8 FOUNDATIONAL KEYS FOR A PERSISTENT MIND:

1. **An unwaveringness of purpose:** Knowing what you want and when you want it is a sure way to build a persistent mind. When purpose isn't known, abuse is inevitable.
2. **A strong passion:** Another word for passion is desire. When you have desire, it will be easier to maintain your persistency. The proof of passion is pursuit.
3. **A strong self-confidence:** You cannot succeed if you don't believe in yourself. The belief in one's ability is essential for success, and persistency is built on that persuasion. To build a good self-reliant mind, learn to work self-affirmation. Talk to yourself. All great minds talk to themselves. Self talk builds the faith necessary to persist.
4. **Specialized game plan:** All plans encourage persistency. Let me add this here; it is not enough to have a plan. Winners know how to execute their plans. Execution is the key. When you begin to execute the plan, the plan will execute your failures and enemies.
5. **Specialized knowledge:** General knowledge can be useless. Study what you need to know to fulfill your plans

for success. Read books about being a better spouse and/or parent if you want a better home. Read books about finances if you desire more money.

6. **Agreement to the plan:** Harmony is essential. Dale Carnegie would fire anyone who disturbed the harmony of his office, no matter how much money they produced for him. His persuasion was that if you break my harmony, you confuse my mind from achieving its goals. Disagreement in your mind creates wrong questions and fear. These are the enemies to persistency.

7. **Will power:** There is a big difference between wanting something and the willingness to do what it takes to have it. You must work the power of your will. Even God doesn't force people to change.

8. **Daily routine:** Some call this habit. I can tell what you're becoming by what you are doing daily. What you are doing daily is deciding what you are becoming permanently. The mind absorbs and becomes a part of the daily experiences upon which it feeds. What diet have you placed your mind on? What are you feeding your brain? Fear, lack, worry, doubt, negative talk, foolish fables and gossip are diets full of unwanted and useless calories.

Take an inventory in your mind right now. See if you are working this master key. If not, I can tell you why you are not succeeding in life.

If I had allowed crisis and situations of others to decide my life, I would have still been living in my past. I would probably be working a menial job and clocking time for a paycheck; but I'm not. I am living my dreams, not my nightmares. I graduated from high school with a GPA of 1.944, was molested from ages 8–12 years old and had terrible fear issues. But I persisted and I won the battle.

23 THINGS THAT WILL KILL PERSISTENCY:

1. The failure to recognize and clearly define one's goals and wants.
2. Procrastination.
3. Unwillingness to read.
4. Indecision.
5. Unwilling to take responsibility for one's own actions.
6. The need to be noticed outweighs the need to get started.
7. Self-Gratification.
8. An argumentative spirit.
9. Always blaming others for your failure.
10. Weakness of passion and desire.
11. The willingness to quit at the first sign of opposition.
12. Not having an organized plan to win.
13. Hesitation; not moving quicker into opportunity.
14. Not understanding the difference between wishing and willingness.
15. Compromise.
16. Trying to find shortcuts to success.
17. Fear of criticism.
18. Fear of failure.
19. Allowing the opinions of others to be stronger than your own decisions.
20. Un-teachable spirit.
21. Having no vision.
22. Quitting.
23. Always thrown off course at the smallest storm.

There is a power that is given to a person who wields the sword of persistency. The capability of winning in times of crisis is persistency's greatest asset. Does the quality of persistence produce some form of spiritual, mental or chemical activity, which gives access to supernatural forces? Does infinite

> **Those Who Have Endured, Have the Right to Be Heard!**

intelligence throw itself on the side of the person who still fights on, after the battle has been lost with the whole world on the opposing side? When you study history you will find that the most successful people all possessed the master key of persistency.

The early martyred Christians had it when they were commanded to give up their faith to live. When they were given the choice to live or die, they chose death. Kings have won great empires with it. Jesus possessed it when he faced the Roman soldiers. He insisted on carrying His destiny on His back so that you and I could be free men and women of God.

THREE FEET FROM WEALTH

Every person is guilty of this mistake at some time or another. I read an interesting story that illustrates this fact. The uncle of R.U. Darby was caught up with "gold fever" in the gold rush days. He went west on a search for gold. He staked his claim and with a pickaxe and shovel, he began his adventure of discovering gold and growing rich. The going was hard, but the desire for gold was stronger than the pain in his back for working night and day. After weeks of hard labor he was finally rewarded for his efforts.

He had discovered the shiny yellow nugget called gold. What he needed now was machinery so he could make himself rich. He covered his mine and went home to Williamsburg, Maryland, and told his relatives and a few friends of the "strike." They invested in the dreams of R.U. Darby's uncle and on his return to the mine, R.U. Darby went with him.

The first large car was mined and sent to a smelter. The returns proved they had struck one of the richest mines in Colorado!

Their idea was to mine and pay off every one they owed including their investors. They would keep the rest for themselves. That's exactly what they did! They worked like dogs day and night to pay off all their debts and investors. The rest was going to make them wealthy. However, the unexpected happened.

They ran out of the gold vein. They had come to the end of their rainbow and the pot of gold was no longer there. They drilled on and on desperately trying to pick up the vein again... all to no avail.

Finally, they decided to quit! They sold the machinery to a junk man for a few hundred dollars and took the train back home feeling defeated and depressed. They were thinking, at least they didn't owe anyone.

Some junk men would have just torn down the machinery and sold the iron for scrap metal. Not this one. He decided to call a mining engineer to look at the mine before he took down the equipment. The engineer's report concluded that the project had failed, not because there wasn't any more gold in the land, but because the first owners didn't understand how gold veins run. The engineer's calculation discovered that a new gold vein would **be found just three feet from where Mr. Darby and his uncle had stopped**.

That "junk man" took millions of dollars in gold ore out of that mine because he got mentorship from an expert. He found out more information before he decided to give up on the mine.

He dug into the mind to unlock the mine!

Imagine stopping three feet from your harvest! Mr. Darby regrouped and became a millionaire in life insurance. They asked him years later how he became so wealthy selling life insurance. His reply, "My 'quit-ability' created my 'stick-ability!' When he found out that he had given up just three feet from the richest gold vein in Colorado, he decided that he would never quit anything again.[vii]

Most of the successful people became that way after they were at the end of their ropes and ready to throw in the towel. Their greatest increase...their greatest harvest came right after that season. Their decision to stick with it and their persistency paid off in the end. Failure is very cunning. It takes pleasure in tricking men to think they are going to fail. Failure loves to dish out a season of frustration right before it's about to release the pay off!

God seems to gravitate to those who will not give up. He loves an achiever, a person who believes enough to keep trying.

I graduated from high school in 1980. There was a call to ministry on my life and God was leading me to go to Bible College. I was perplexed in my spirit because I had a terrible GPA (grade point average) of 1.944.

I had a reading disability, dyslexia, which caused me to become behind in reading. I was reading around the eighth grade level as a senior in high school.

I applied for Bible College in 1981 and I had to beg the school to accept me. I was so pumped and excited. I was following God's call and going to college. At the end of my first semester, after much studying and praying, I made D's and F's with a GPA 1.9! I got the same results the second semester. I even took a class that taught how to study effectively hoping that it would help me read and comprehend better. I had so much desire and passion to learn and to make better grades. Sometimes passion and desire are not enough.

The Dean of the school called me into his office one day and informed me that if I did not raise my GPA to a 2.0, I would be expelled. I will never forget that day driving home, stunned and confused. I walked into my house, fell on my face and cried so hard. My head was aching; my mind was tormented. **Why would God bring me here to fail?** I began to ask the Lord why He was doing this to me.

I made up my mind that I wasn't going back. While I was laying there deciding on my next move, the Lord spoke to my spirit and this was His comment to my mind; *"Whatever you do son, don't quit! Don't you give up! Go back this last semester and you give it all you've got. If they want to, they can kick you out, but don't you quit. Son, with me **ENDURANCE IS A QUALIFIER!"***

I decided right then not to quit. I signed up for one more semester. I decided to give it one more try.

Something happened that semester. God began to heal my mind. I started comprehending and understanding what I was studying. I began making A's and B's on every test.   At the end of that semester, I made all A's and one B! My GPA was a 3.25!

While I am writing this, I'm looking at the plaque on my wall that says, The Dean's List Certificate. I made the national Dean's List. I have seen God do so many wonderful and awesome things with my life, all because I refused to quit and to endure.

Someone reading this right now is about three feet from your **pay off**! Don't give up…

CHAPTER NINE

"IMAGINATION"
THE WINDOW TO
RESTORATION

"You see things; and you say, 'Why?' But I dream things that never were; and I say, 'Why not?'" George Bernard

"Limitations live only in our minds. But if we use our imaginations, our possibilities become limitless."
Jamie Paolinetti

"What the mind can conceive and the mind can believe the mind can achieve." Napoleon Hill

Thoughts are things. Think for a second. Everything around you was a thought before it was a thing. Someone once asked Thomas Edison how he made so many great inventions. His answer was, *"Thoughts are things."* Nothing in the earth got here until it was first conceived in the world of thought. The mind's ability to dream is its greatest asset.

Thomas Edison believed the mind was made up of the same matter as the universe. He believed when God placed the brain in our heads, He made it out of the same stuff that He made the universe from. I like to take that thought a little further. I believe we are made in the image of God and that our minds were made in God's image. Thus, Mr. Edison had the right idea; he just called it wrong. It is not the universe; it is God.

"So God created man in his own image, in the image of God he created him; male and female he created them." Genesis 1:27 NIV

I don't believe we were mere amoebas that climbed out of a cesspool millions of years ago. It takes more faith to believe in evolution than in creation. To believe that humans *"just happened"* or *"evolved"* from a primitive ape is mere ridiculous.

Let me tell you a quick reason why I believe in the value of your existence and why you are more than what you think. There are over 75 trillion cells in your body and each one of those 75 trillion cells carries a strand of DNA that has over 3 billion characters that describe who you are. These are your own personal code and no one has the same. Each one of the 75 trillion cells has a strand of DNA that contains 3 billion characters. If you stretched those 3 billion characters horizontally, it would be at least 6 feet long. If you read day and night, with no rest or sleep, it would take you 96 years to read what God has encoded in your life, your purpose and your make up. WOW! You truly are fearfully and wonderfully made.

A God guided life is a life that understands the value of the mind. Your mind is the place where dreams are made, and imagination is the vehicle where ideas are birthed and formed.

Man's only limitation, within reason, lies in the development and use of imagination. I want you to center your attention on the development of your imagination. This is the faculty that you will use more often in the process of converting desire into money and transforming the intangible impulse of desire into the tangible reality of wealth. Success calls for the use of a plan. These plans must be formed with the help of the imagination and mainly with the mind that can dream bigger than its present circumstances.

> **The Only Way to Leave Your Present and Enter Your Future is Through Your Imagination**

Everything we are experiencing and enjoying in life - cars, airplanes, cell phones, computers, and anything else you can think of - all started in the hall ways and corridors of someone's imagination.

Men were once arrested for even thinking we could fly. Now, we can eat breakfast in New York City, drive to the airport, board a jet, fly to the west coast and eat lunch in California. What once took months and maybe even a year, we now can do within hours.

This is big in me. "THOUGHTS ARE THINGS!" I was waking up one morning and my mind was saying to me, '**Your thoughts have presence.**' Over and over again my mind kept saying this to me as if it were trying to free itself to be more and create more. My subconscious mind was screaming to me, *"Believe!"* What things in my life have I missed because I refused to allow my imagination to run free?

We are conditioned to build our lives around memories. Our whole existence is usually thinking about where we've been.

Look around your office, look around your house. More than likely, the pictures on your walls tell the story of where you have been. They are walls of memorials. Point to me your dream wall, your imagination wall!

We can't build a business, we can't build wealth and we can't do anything until we can first dream it.

Definition of the word imagination: *The act or power of forming mental images of what is not actually present, the act or power of creating mental images of what has never been actually experienced or of creating new images or ideas by combining previous experience; creative power.*[viii]

What is the Enemy to a Dreamer? Someone Else's Experience

Once again we are confronted with the word "creative." The Bible says that you and I are created in the image and likeness of God. I believe that God put the power to create, more than the power to compete, within all of us. When the mind is taken over with entitlement thinking, we become enslaved to a welfare mind.

This is exactly what happened to the children of Israel when they were in slavery for 450 years to the Egyptians. God heard their cries and decided to free them from that place. Freedom wasn't just about taking the shackles off their feet and hands. What good is freeing you from a space if you are still mentally bound to that place? It doesn't matter if I can get you out physically if you're still mentally bound. **"Your mind is your world."** The world you live in is not the world you really live in. The world you think you live in is really where you live. I know that sounds like a play on words, but read it slowly and think about it. You are only as strong as you think you are in any given situation and crisis. It took God forty years to attempt to change the children of Israel's mindset. Finally, He just let them die out and allowed their offspring to conquer and live in the promise.

This happened simply because those who lived in slavery couldn't get the entitlement mind changed over to an empowerment mind set.

Don't allow anyone to ruin your dreams. Without a dream your future is bleak. Your present is permanent. Sit down and write down your dreams. Do it right now! Stop everything and document your future.

24 THINGS THAT HINDER YOUR IMAGINATION PROCESS:

1. Wrong people
2. Those who trivialize your passion
3. Negative talk and negative people
4. Resisting the power to day dream
5. Lack of knowledge
6. Lack of vision
7. Worry
8. Stress
9. Fatigue
10. Poor health
11. Doubt
12. Lack of faith
13. Fear
14. Un-forgiveness
15. Bitterness
16. Racism
17. Discouragement
18. Strife
19. Confusion
20. Religion
21. Ignorance
22. Lack of passion
23. Unknown purpose
24. Overlooked opportunities

18 FACTS ABOUT IMAGINATION

1. You will always move in the direction of your strongest and most dominate thought.
2. Your imagination is an invisible machine inside your mind that creates pictures of something in your future.
3. Uncommon achievers have learned how to use their imagination effectively.
4. Miracles begin in the soil of your imagination.
5. Abraham used his imagination to strengthen his faith.
6. God even acknowledged the power of an imagination (Genesis 11:6).
7. God has given every one of us this incredible gift.
8. Imagination can unleash unexpected energy.
9. Jesus used his imagination to picture the future of his suffering. He had to believe in the resurrection.
10. Winning athletes use their imaginations to be winners.
11. Your imagination controls you!
12. It is your responsibility to protect your mind and imagination.
13. You can change disaster seeds into dream seeds in the world of your imagination.
14. Your imagination's mate is your memory.
15. You can begin using your imaginations productively today… don't delay.
16. You can change what has been happening in your life by focusing your imagination to something better.
17. Refuse to misuse your imagination.
18. Imagination is the factory where your future grows.

Imagination is the factory for your future. Without a dream you have no hope for tomorrow. I said it at the beginning of this chapter and I want to drive it home here. You can't leave your present unless you have an imagination.

All things on the earth came from one powerful thought. God used His thinking power to create in a dark and formless substance. *The earth was without form and void (Genesis 1).* God decided to take formless substance and place His words that came from his thoughts to it; thus formless became formed substance.

I believe we have that same power. We can speak into our future and command formlessness to "become." We can create with our imagination. Don't spend your life competing with others. Spend your life growing your mind and imagination so that you can create the world you want to live in.

Take possession of your own mind.

CHAPTER TEN

"DECISIONS"
THE POWER
TO RECOVERY

*"A wise man makes his own **decisions**; an ignorant man follows public opinion."* Chinese Proverb

*"More than anything else, I believe it's our **decisions**, not the conditions of our lives that determine our destiny."* Anthony Robbins

*F*ailure is inevitable to people who can't make up their own mind. Indecision is the highway for failure, the bridge for defeat and the ingredient to a miserable life. A very powerful tool in life is a made up mind.

YOUR MIND IS YOUR WORLD

More gold has been mined out of the mind of men than dug out of the earth. Men spend a lot of time and energy looking for what they are unwilling to see. The key to everything is within. God placed in every human the power to create their world and that power is in the mind. Something we are not seeing is keeping us bound to what we already see. I can't make right decisions if I can't see. The power to subdue is attached to the ability to see. You can't subdue what you can't see! My mind is my world. This powerful principle seems to be an important subject in most of my books. I believe the power of the mind is the most overlooked power we possess.

- We can have...
- We can do...
- We can be...whatever we think we can!

The Power of Awareness

What have you ignored lately? I recently purchased a new Yamaha 242 boat. I did have a Nautica boat, but after I purchased the Yamaha it seems like I see Yamaha boats all over the lake. I have spent so much time on the lake and never noticed them before. My mind wasn't aware of this type of boat because it wasn't awakened in my reality.

This scenario happens all the time. When we wake up our awareness, things that we haven't seen for years now become apparent. It's always been there; we just weren't aware of it. Could you be missing out on something great simply because you have refused to look and dig in your own mind and thoughts? Have you allowed voices to be louder than your own thoughts? Our decisions are persuaded by our minds. If we aren't confident in our own minds we will live in the center of indecisions. This will propel us into a life where we can never recover what we've lost. Our recovery is dependent on our decision-making abilities.

Don't get down; don't get discouraged. Everyone is confident in their decisions until someone questions them. For

> **Everyone is Confident in Their Decisions Until Someone Questions Them.**

instance, one day I was traveling down the interstate with my wife. I knew exactly where I was going and had been to the place many times. While travelling at the speed of 65 mph, I put on my blinker to exit off the interstate to my destination. No sooner than I began to exit the flow of traffic when my wife looked over at me and said, **"Are you sure?"** All of a sudden my confident decision went out the window. I jerked the car back into the traffic, looked at her and said, "Why? Do you know something I don't?"

She looked at me and said, "No, just wanted to make sure."

This question created delayment in our arrival to the destination. We were stuck in traffic and had to go at least five miles the wrong way just to exit and turn around to go back to the right exit.

I was confident until questioned.

These master keys are very important. You can't go forward in life, in your finances or in your business without a strong decision making process. My mentor shared a very powerful key with me, "Decisions decide wealth."

Put any word in the place of wealth. Decisions decide joy.... decisions decide relationships... decisions decide access...

promotion… education… consequences.

Wrong decisions trigger the law of unintended consequences. A lot of the stuff that is happening in our world has nothing to do with God. I can guarantee that most of the crisis we are facing can be traced back to our wrong decisions. People who are struggling financially are usually victims of their own bad decisions. God isn't doing all this stuff; we are. We just don't want to man up! We are afraid to admit that we could be the problem. Let me illustrate.

A young teenager climbs into the car with his friend; both have been drinking at a party. Neither should be in the car; however, overlooking truth, they decide to drive home. Driving at illegal speeds, the teenage driver loses control of the car, slams it into a tree and both are killed. Now, someone will ask, *"Why did God let this happen?"*

> **Wrong Decisions Trigger the Law of Unintended Consequences.**

God did not let this happen. They gambled. They tried, but they came up that night wanting. *Their wrong decision triggered the law of unintended consequences.* This wasn't God's decision. This wasn't God's doing. This was the power of their wrong decision.

Decisions are the master key of wealth. They are also the master key of failure.

Let me give you some important life decisions.

THE ACCESS YOU DECIDE TO PURSUE

The right access can accelerate your success rate. The wrong access can delay your success. Access is very important. You must understand that access has to be pursued. Those who are ahead of you are not going to enter your season simply because you believe you deserve their help.

Access has to be pursued. What you are unwilling to pursue you do not qualify to receive. *Access is as valuable as money.* The definition of welfare is to sit and wait for someone to come along and get you out. *It's the mindset that someone owes you.* No one owes you anything. I believe welfare is destroying America. Do you desire to win? Do you want to live your life beyond the boundaries of mediocrity? Have you had enough of your life and level of living? Then you must pursue access! Find someone worth pursuing. Serve them... honor them... respect them. They will open their heart and mind to you. The decision to pursue access is a major decision. Don't enter this decision without much thought and prayer.

Access provides information that would otherwise be off limits. I have gained so much wisdom by being allowed certain access. I've met CEO's and Presidents of major television stations and corporations because of access. I have been able to sit at the table with some of the world's greatest influencers. Access is very important for your life to advance to the next place.

Decisions may give you access, but it will be protocol that keeps you there. It can be easy to enter the palace. The gift in life is not just getting in, but being allowed to stay. Protocol is defined as knowing how to act in the presence of greatness.

Some call protocol conduct. Every season has a code of conduct to enter it. If you refuse to find what that code is, then your present season will remain permanent.

THE FRIENDSHIPS YOU DECIDE TO KEEP

Not everyone around you belongs around you.

THOSE WHO CANNOT DISCERN YOUR WORTH DISQUALIFY FOR YOUR FRIENDSHIP.

This is not an easy decision, especially if you have my personality and love to have people around you. I have discovered in 25 years of ministry that allowing access to those who have not earned it has cost me more than anything.

Those whom you allow access to your conversations, those whom you allow access into your private life and those whom you allow access into your home must qualify. The access you allow can be revealing something that you would want to keep hidden from your enemy.

Let me caution you! Not everyone around you is serving you because they respect you. There are those whom you have allowed access that are your enemy in hiding. They are merely awaiting the exposure of a weakness to bring you down. Qualify everyone! Do background checks on those who claim they want to serve you.

PEOPLE YOU ARE UNABLE TO INFLUENCE:

- Those who think you are their problem.
- Those who do not value what you have deemed important.
- Those who refuse to let you mentor them.
- Those who ignore your instructions.
- Those who weaken your faith.
- Those who hate what you love.
- Those who are comfortable sitting at your enemies table.
- Those who do not defend you in your absence.
- Those who refuse to support your vision financially.
- Those who believe they know more than you.
- Those who get jealous over your blessings.
- Those who refuse to honor you with gifts.
- Those who see you as their friend or family.
- Those who will not recognize the gifts God has placed in you.
- Those who cannot take correction.
- Those who refuse to tithe.
- Those who refuse to change.
- Those who are unwilling to admit they need you.
- Those who are comfortable in the presences of the ungodly.
- Those who are willing to expose your weakness.

This is a powerful list. I only wish I would have understood this earlier in my ministry. I would have saved myself years of heartache and grief.

Stop trying to win the world and start changing those who are assigned to you. Only allow access to those who have been assigned to you.

THE DREAM THAT YOU DECIDE TO MAKE YOUR OBSESSION

You must decide what dream you are willing to make your focus. How do you kill a visionary? Give him more than one dream. The more dreams you have, the harder it will be to stay focused.

What is a dream? *A fanciful vision of the conscious mind; a fond hope or aspiration, images of thoughts passing through the psyche.*

A dream is the power to leave your present place and enter a world that is only controlled by your fears and doubts. When you dream, the sky is the limit. I've often said to those around me, *"If you are going to dream, leave your check book at home."*

What dream have you made your obsession? What dream have you tabled or shelved because someone told you it was impossible? There have been so many times in my ministry that I've stared into the hollow eyes of others who have allowed life's circumstances to abort the dreams of their youth. They have accepted their life and settled in to what they have allowed to happen; a marriage, a child, a mortgage payment, a car payment... These things don't have to rob you of your ability to dream! What would life be like void of a dream? I'll tell you; **hollow and empty**! I cannot imagine what it would be like to be unable to dream.

- *A dream is the only way to exit your crisis for a brief moment.*
- *A dream is the only way to visit another place or time.*
- *A dream is the only world where you don't need money or education to succeed.*

There was a movie that came out years ago entitled **"THE FIELD OF DREAMS."** The voice in that movie would say over and over. *"If you build it, they will come."* Well I want to say if you dream it and believe it, you can have it.

Without a dream, you can never have a vision, and without a vision, you will never enter your future.

WHAT DO YOU DREAM ABOUT?

Many people will enter into some form of a business at least once in their lifetime. Some of you have entered into network marketing to do a home based business. This can be your greatest door to enter into a financial life style that you have always wanted to live in.

You can't build any business unless you have built in your heart a dream to where you want that business to be.

The only way to exit your present and enter your future is with an imagination. Without a dream, you will never have an imagination. It cost nothing to dream. It doesn't require education or mentorship to dream. We would spend hours daydreaming when we were children. No one taught us how to do that. Do you remember what you wanted to be when you were a child? When you are a child, everyone tells you to stop dreaming and face reality. When you grow up, people tell you to dream again. No wonder life can be confusing.

Dream! You are not going to build your business without a dream. What do you want to drive? What kind of house would you live in if money wasn't an issue? Where would you go on vacation if you could afford to go anywhere? All of these questions require a dream. Start dreaming and begin to live again in your mind.

The enemy to a dream is someone else's experience. Don't allow someone else's experience in life to stop you from dreaming and believing in your future. Walk away quickly from those who try to sabotage your dreams. Someone once asked me, *"Would you like to know who your enemy is today?"* I replied,

"Yes!" They said, *"Then begin to announce your dreams and immediately, I promise, your enemy will materialize."*

Your enemies are those who speak against your dreams and imaginations. They will be the people that you would have never expected. It may be your best friend, your parents or someone you have trusted. Stop talking to these people about your dreams. Only talk to those who will be happy for your vision.

CHAPTER ELEVEN

"OPPORTUNITY"
THE DOOR TO RESTORATION

"Opportunity is missed by most people because it is dressed in overalls and looks like work." Thomas Edison

"I will prepare and some day my chance will come." Abraham Lincoln

*O*pportunity doesn't go away; it only moves to another. Many have been scheduled for success but haven't experienced it yet because of missed opportunity. It's not that opportunity wasn't present, but that they failed to recognize the season of opportunity. No one is going to live a **Guided by God Life** until they learn to recognize opportunity.

Opportunity is defined as *an uncertain event with a positive probable consequence. Related to risk. The possibility that one or more individuals or organizations will experience beneficial consequences from an event or circumstance.*

"Opportunity will rarely call upon you in the moment of your choice."

If you recognize this quote, you probably have watched the movie "Transformers." I loved this saying because it is so true. You rarely get to pick how opportunity will be revealed to you. You can only decide if you will seize the moment.

CRISIS IS USUALLY OPPORTUNITY

Opportunity is almost always disguised in a crisis or a problem. Many fail to see the door of opportunity because all they see is the wall of problems or crisis that besets them. Someone once said that most millionaires became millionaires in the time of their darkest hours. It was when they were losing everything that they found the real faith to persist, and in those times they discovered the law of opportunity. I am reminded of a story when Thomas Edison was attempting to invent the light bulb. It took Mr. Edison and his assistant ten thousand tries and each one ended with no success. The story is related that after the ten thousandth time the assistant became very discouraged and angry.

He was heard saying to Mr. Edison, *"We are failures..."*

Thomas looked at his assistant and said, *"Son, on the contrary; we are not failures. Don't you realize that we are the only two people on the earth that know ten thousand ways of how not to make a light bulb?"* It was on their next attempt that they discovered the filament that would become the light bulb. The opportunity was hidden in the trial of failure. Many would have quit after a few hundred tries. The difference between the wealth of success and the failure of it is how you push past the problems, defeat and pain to seize the opportunity. It is almost always hidden in those rare times you want to quit.

Opportunity rarely calls on us in moments that we choose. David went on the battlefield, not expecting to fight a giant but to complete an instruction his father gave him. Instead of delivering food to his brothers, the opportunity presented itself to face a giant. The difference between failure and promotion is **what you see and how swiftly you move** to seize the opportunity that is presented. Be very cautious at listening to those who only see the problem. They can be the voice that talks you into fear and moves you away from your opportunity. The men said, *"Have you seen this man...?"*

Yes, I've seen him! But what I see is not a problem, but a promotion. What I see is not a wall, but a door. What I see is not defeat, but rewards. What I see is a season of change facing me, and all I have to do is face it and conquer it. When I succeed, I will change the season of my life with one moment of opportunity. I will move from living in the fields to living in the palace.

*"And all the men of Israel, when they saw the man, fled from him and were dreadfully afraid. So the men of Israel **said**, Have you seen this man who has come up? Surely he has come up to defy Israel..." 1 Samuel 17:24-25 NKJV*

The biggest secret to opportunity is learning how to assess the moment. Don't allow the moment to be consumed by your problem, pain or crisis. Stop, look, pray and listen. The moment may reveal the opportunity that is hidden in it. David stopped to listen to the giant. Hearing the giant defy His God angered him.

That alone was enough for David to stand up and defend the honor of His faith and His God. When David heard how this Philistine was talking he knew that something had to be done.

Questions are the doors that reveal a problem as an opportunity.

"Then David spoke to the men who stood by him, saying, What shall be done for the man who kills this Philistine and takes away the reproach from Israel? For who is this uncircumcised Philistine, that he should defy the armies of the living God?" 1 Samuel 17:26 NKJV

This is a very important key! Ask questions before you make a decision. David saw the problem just like everyone else. Then David asked the question that revealed the hidden opportunity in the crisis. *"What shall be done for the man who wins?"*

Opportunity is an Invitation to Change

Who faces this problem and beats it? Look at this master mind-set. **For who is this uncircumcised enemy, that he should defy my belief system.** *(Paraphrased)* WOW! What faith! The ability to see something different than others causes you to move beyond the norm and into the abnormal river of increase and wealth.

Position yourself to be seen by opportunity.

It's not enough that you can recognize an opportunity. It's not enough that you can seize the moment and position yourself to be in the room or area where opportunity is passing by. There is one more thing we must do to capture and move into the season of opportunity. We must position ourselves to be seen by opportunity when it arrives.

When Jesus was entering a city, the crowd had gathered to see Him. Wherever Jesus went, circumstances changed and the people realized that incredible power and blessings rested with Him. People will always show up when they think opportunity is passing by.

In the crowd, there was a man who couldn't see opportunity because he wasn't tall enough to see over the shoulders of those in front of him. His name was Zacchaeus.

"And when Jesus came to the place, he looked up, and saw him, and said unto him, Zacchaeus, make haste, and come down; for today I must abide at thy house. Luke 19:5 KJV

Zacchaeus decided to do something the crowds weren't doing. He changed his position. He elevated himself by climbing a tree. Decide right now to do what the crowd is unwilling to do. Elevate yourself to a place so you can see further down the road to your scheduled opportunity. Jesus looked up and saw a man that was willing to go higher and do more than the average person in the crowd. He elevated himself to see opportunity better than the others.

Opportunity is the invitation to change. What are you willing to do to have opportunity notice you?

Think what would have happened if Zacchaeus hadn't climbed that tree? He would have lived his life in the norm and never experienced the season of change. He saw opportunity coming and decided to position himself, not just to only see opportunity but to also increase his chances for opportunity to see him.

The Bible is a Book of the Unusual

The Bible is a book of the unusual. I can't think of one story or one instruction in the Bible that fits in the norm or the usual.

- It's unusual for someone to build an Ark in the desert and wait for rain that has never happened before.
- It's unusual for three men to throw themselves into a fiery furnace.

- It's unusual for 300 men to face an enemy that out numbers them 1000 to one. Gideon depleted his army simply because God said he had too many. Gideon didn't think he had enough. God is a God of the unusual.
- It's unusual for a father to take his only son to a mountain to offer him as a sacrifice simply because God asked for it.
- It's unusual for a man to take a beating from a Roman soldier, carry a cross, take the ridicule of all the people, for that man to be nailed to that cross to hang for hours, when He could have called 10,000 angels to rescue him from it. In case you don't know, this was JESUS.
- It's unusual for a man to die, in three days come out of death and walk out of the grave to sit and rule on a throne.

The Bible is a book of the unusual. If you keep doing what you usually do, don't be shocked when you keep getting what you usually get.

THE WAY YOU APPROACH THE BIBLE IS IMPORTANT

PRESENCE: God is very meticulous on how he wants us to approach certain things. He was specific on how we are to approach Him. We are to enter His gates with thanksgiving and enter His courts with praise. Make your supplications after you've spent time in thanksgiving and praise. Come into His presence with the right attitude and singing. I believe that when we work out this approach that by the time we get to God's ear, there won't be much left to ask for. In His presence, you will discover all you need to be healed and to win.

WORD OF GOD: When we approach the Word of God there are some things we need to be aware of:

- Partial truth is dangerous.
- Denominational truth is blinding.
- Religious truth is deadly.

- Perceived truth is false truth.
- Jesus is the only truth!

Any truth received outside of Jesus and off the foundation of His wisdom is divisive. Truth that is laced with human opinion can become the most dangerous truth of all. The Bible is God's word and that Word is Jesus. You may become blind, religious and use the Bible as your book to judge others instead of grow and judge yourself if you read the Bible without looking for Christ. The truth is no one really wants truth. Truth will always expose the lies. If the lies of your life aren't exposed then you have received a gospel that isn't Christ.

Three things will happen when Christ's spirit enters a room. First, lies are exposed. Second, the religious become irritated, and third, change will happen.

There are two things we must know about approaching God's Word, the Bible. First, we must have the unequivocal persuasion that the Bible is not just a book, but a book that is alive with God's breath and power. The Bible is a living book. This is very important. If it's not alive then it becomes a history book, a book with stories that did happen. It becomes a book with good and encouraging stories but no power.

> **No One Seems to Really Want Truth.**

If it is **ALIVE**, then it just *didn't happen. It is still happening*. The passages are relevant and real to my life. The same God who rescued Daniel from the jaws of hungry lions will rescue me from the jaws that are attempting to eat up all my greatness and life.

I know that the same God who entered the fire for three Hebrew boys and changed it into their safety and promotion is the same God who will enter my fire of tribulation and turn my problem into my promotion. We must understand and believe that the Word of God is a living book; no questions!

Second, we must understand that there is no word in Hebrew or Greek that translates into coincidence or accident. Events didn't just happen "accidently" in the Bible. There was a plan and a purpose for all things that happened.

The things that are going on in the world around us today are not shocking to God. Every living and created thing on planet earth reveals to us that there is a divine force, an intelligent being, a God who designed it all. There is an architect over all creation and man. The word architect means *"ancient one."* There is an eternal being that has existed longer than anyone or anything erected around us.

Just as an architect is able to envision buildings and monuments before a foundation is poured or one brick is laid, there is an architect and designer over your life. Nothing is accidental, especially when it comes to you. You are not an accident. God, the Ancient One, has a plan and a purpose for you.

To understand how this works you have to know your position on the earth and God's position in heaven.

Your position is--RECOVERY.
God's position is--RESTORATION.

You will never be able to be restored if you have not positioned yourself for recovery. When we do not involve God in our lives we make stupid decisions that cost us a lot of good things. Everyone experiences loss.

The cross is the door to the Son of God. The cross is where you lift your hands and confess your weaknesses, foolishness and stupid decisions. After you've confessed, posture yourself to wait on God. This puts you in the position for RECOVERY.

Remember, Jesus receives your confessions and takes them to the Father. The Father is scheduling your recovery through Christ. Sometimes this may feel like a long time, but time is irrelevant with God.

He does this through the power of **RESTORATION**. God is doing a new thing and in you it shall be born. Say that right now. Say, *"My God is doing a new thing; in me it will be born."* Remember not the things of old, for God is doing a new thing.
Restoration means getting back what you've lost and

more. When God restores, you become more than what you were originally meant to be. Restoration in the natural is putting something back to its original state but with God it is more! Let me put it this way. If you bought a 1967 Chevy in 1967 it would cost you around $2000.00. If you take that car out of a junkyard and restore it to its original state, it would be worth around $50,000.00. Restoration is more!

Sometimes we don't understand why we have to go through struggles and crises. God knew He was going to come into your life and pull you out of the junkyard of 'hurt and abuse, left for dead and useless'. He knew that He would take you in His garage of love and power to restore to you those things that life had abused in you. You are worth more now than you were in your past because of restoration!

I believe that nothing is accidental or coincidental. There is a purpose for what you have been through. You survived it for a reason. Your mess will become your message. Take your mess and add age to it.....mess plus age equals **MESSAGE** (MESS+AGE= Message).

Don't miss any more opportunities. Remember, opportunities are almost always disguised as a problem or opposition. The opposition you are willing to face will be the door of opportunity you are about to walk through.

CHAPTER TWELVE

CAN YOUR REACTION STAND TRIAL?

REACTION CAN DECIDE THE LONGEVITY OF
YOUR RECOVERY

7 believe that I Peter 5:8-10 is a testament from Peter

on how we must act after we've been through trials. Look at these verses. I believe that the gospel is really about how Peter was restored after he failed to stand up for Christ and denied Him three times.

*"Be __sober,__ be __vigilant__; because __your adversary__ the devil, as a roaring lion, walketh about, seeking whom he may devour: Whom resist stedfast in the faith, **knowing that the same afflictions are accomplished in your brethren that are in the world**. But the God of all grace, who hath called us unto his eternal glory by Christ Jesus, after that ye have suffered a while, make you perfect, stablish, strengthen, settle you." I Peter 5:8-10 KJV*

Pay attention to some of the words in this passage and grasp a deeper meaning of what Peter was actually referring to. The first word is *"sober."* Be sober, or a better translated word is be *"self-controlled."* The next word is *"Be vigilant."* I like the Greek meaning which is to be "watchful!"

Most people read this passage with their focus on the phrase that talks about our adversary seeking to devour. We enter unnecessary warfare when we make this part of the scripture our focus. I don't believe that Peter wanted us to make the adversary our focus.

I believe our focus should be monitoring our "self-control"…"**Be sober, be vigilant**". Our warfare should be over are reactions in times of attack. The adversary is walking around us, not attacking us but watching us. He is monitoring how we react in times of trial and testing. Our behavior is giving us away.

Who better to write this than Peter? Knowing what he had to live through when Jesus was crucified and how quickly he reacted wrongly when he was being challenged to stand. Also, think of all the other times Peter reacted. He cut off the ear of a man in the garden out of his anger. It seems that Peter was always speaking up and making negative or controversial comments. We are so much like Peter. Think of how many times we have failed; how many times we didn't make the right stand when we knew we should have. We hide our faith when we are supposed to shine it. We are more like Peter than we would like to admit.

"But the God of all grace, who hath called us unto his eternal glory by Christ Jesus, after that you have suffered a while, make you perfect, stablished, strengthen, and settle you." I Peter 5:10 KJV

Wow! What a different person. Peter was giving the grace to others that he received through his failure. I like the NIV version of this verse:

"And the God of all grace, who called you to his eternal glory in Christ, after you have suffered a little while, will himself restore you and make you strong, firm and steadfast." I Peter 5:10

"... God..., will himself restore you." Praise God! God's primary purpose is to restore the fallen, the broken, the hurting and the lost. God always restores with interest. Restored and more!

Four things the restored can expect:

1. **Perfected:** I can expect to be much better off than when I failed. I know that there's something about restoration that gives me a better understanding to my flesh. I believe once you have fallen and survived, it will be hard to fall in that area of your life again. By this, you have been made perfect. God births distaste for failure in you after you have been restored so that you will never want to return to that place.

2. **Established:** When you decide to return, you're not coming back to just float around and try to fit in. No, you will return with more purpose and more grace than when you failed. To be established means to settle in a position

or a place. Your return builds in you a mindset of "I belong." Until you believe you belong, you will always be misled. There's a powerful healing in the mind when you know you belong. You will never leave your present until you believe you belong in your future. You are never going to advance until you believe you belong in better. I know this first hand. I know how it feels to believe you don't belong; but I also know the power of self-healing that comes when you begin to believe you do belong. You belong in a debt free home. You belong in a better home. You belong driving a new car. You belong in your church! There's a power in the understanding of belonging. Are you willing to fight to be in a season of the place you belong in?

There is no warfare for your season of next if you don't believe you belong where your enemy is. This is why God brought the children of Israel to a land that was occupied by an enemy. God was training and changing their mindset. They needed to develop a warrior's persuasion instead of a slavery persuasion. If you aren't willing to fight for it, you may not believe it belongs to you.

3. **Strength:** When you are restored you are strengthened. You are not just getting what you have lost back in restoration; you are getting your mind back. When your mind is healed, you are healed. Restoration is like exercising your muscles. When you are restored for much, you believe your worth to be that much and more.

4. **Settle you:** Sin loses its luster when you've decided to settle where you are supposed to be. I believe one of the major reasons so many leave church and never commit is because they have a restless spirit. Divorce is at an all time high. Why? People are not settled. They are always looking to be somewhere else. ***Always be where you are!*** My mentor taught me this many years ago. When you wake up, be in your day. Don't carry yesterday in today. Stop trying to be in your tomorrow; live in your today. So

many people are seeking to be in their future that they don't know how to live in their present.

Because of my emotional wounds it was easy for me to try and be somewhere else instead of where I was. I could be sitting at the table with my family and my mind would be somewhere else. I was never able to enjoy the moment because I was always looking for something else in another moment. This robbed me of so many good moments. Have you ever experienced this? Thank God I am restored! You should shout that right now, "I AM RESTORED!"

Let's look at what made Peter so focused on restoration.

*"And the Lord said, "Simon, Simon! Indeed, Satan **has asked for you, that he may sift you as wheat**. But I have prayed for you; that your faith should not fail; and **when you have returned to Me, strengthen your brethren**." Luke 22:31-32*

Wow, get a hold of what happened here. Jesus addressed Peter and let him know that the adversary had asked for him. We need to break this down to grasp it in full detail.

1. **Satan** means accuser. The accuser came before heaven with Peter in his focus. He asked to sift Peter as wheat. One translation says, *"Satan desires you."* The Hebrew meaning is that the enemy has demanded for Peter to be put in account.

2. **Asked** or desire means the accuser is demanding to put you on trial. The enemy wanted to put Peter to the test to see how he would react.

3. **Sifting**… this word has a great meaning. Sift means irregularity. The enemy schedules an irregular moment in your regular schedule that will put you out of sync to your plans. Your reaction will be put on trial when this happens. This is exactly how most of us fall. We fall into drugs or some blatant sin by our reaction to crisis. So

many times I have failed this test! I have failed it, you have failed it and we all know that Peter failed it.

Jesus told Peter this trial was coming and that He was going to pray for him. Jesus didn't pray away the trial nor did He pray that Peter wouldn't fail the test. Jesus prayed that after the test Peter's faith would still stand strong, even after he had failed. Jesus could not stop Peter's failure, and sometimes God does not stop ours. Failure happens, but the key is to keep your faith even after you have fallen. Keep your faith intact, keep seeking truth, and don't allow your faith to be moved or weakened in times of failure. Keep standing strong like Peter did.

Jesus was not focused on Peter's stand, but His return. *"When you have returned to me..."* Jesus isn't focused on our failure but on our ability and willingness to return to Him.

Peter's return has a request attached to it. Jesus asked Peter that when he had returned to strengthen his brothers. He was to be more to them than before he had failed by giving them grace and love. They were going to need it.

REACTION IS IMPORTANT TO GOD

8 THINGS THAT REVEAL YOU:

1. **Conversation**: If you want to know where someone is, listen to them talk. Conversation is more powerful than anyone is telling you. You are living today the conversation you had yesterday. We spend more time talking about what moves and hurts us than what helps and heals us. We love to tell everyone we meet about our pains, our crises, our losses and our struggles. No wonder they never leave. Our conversations are giving them power to keep hanging around. My good friend, Pastor Walter Hallam, says it this way, *"Don't listen to the echoes around you; listen to the revelation that is within you."*

Stop talking so much about the situation and start using the voice of revelation to counter attack your situation. Echoes are nothing more than the voices around you that want to talk about your pain, your losses and your failures. They are those who only focus on your reputation instead of the revelation that God has placed in your situation. Sow the seed of revelation into the mountain of your situation, and let the seed of revelation change the mountain of your situation.

2. **Behavior**: What got you here won't get you there. The difference in exiting your present season is not trying to do the same thing you did in your last season. For instance, look at athletes. After high school the talent gets even stronger. My son played high school football. He was a middle line backer and was pretty good. He was good enough to go and play in a division II college. I'll never forget the day that we drove him to college to begin his football career at the college level. I was so proud and sad at the same time. I knew this was his time to leave the nest and experience life at another level.

It was exciting to go visit him for the first time. He had lost weight and looked so different to me. I asked him *"How's college been treating you son?"*

His answer was, *"Dad, it's nothing like what I expected. College football is nothing like high school football."*

I asked him how it was different. He replied, *"Dad, everyone here hits hard. Everyone here knows the game. In high school only a few really hit hard and gave it all they got. Everyone on the team is talented and gifted. Of course, there are those who are better than others, but all can play the game."*

Think about this for a moment. *What got you here won't get you there!* There is a place in life where everybody can play the game. What separates you from the others will not be skill, but behavior. How you behave becomes the focus. Are you a leader or are you easily led? Behavior reveals you.

This is how the children of Israel got stuck in the wilderness; they couldn't adjust their behavior. What got them out of Egypt wouldn't bring them out of the wilderness. Crying and praying got them out of Egypt.

"And the Lord said, I have surely seen the affliction of my people which are in Egypt, and have heard their cry by reason of their taskmasters; for I know their sorrows;" Exodus 3:7 KJV

God heard their cries; He saw their affliction. He was moved and delivered them from the hand of bondage and the land of bondage. The children of Israel reached the Red Sea with no place to go with the Egyptian army behind them. God told Moses to keep moving forward. By moving forward, God opened the Red Sea, their obstacle, and the children of Israel continued toward their destiny. As long as they were pursuing God's promises, God dealt with the enemy that was behind them.

God will bring you out of the land of bondage. You will experience the hand of God when you are coming out of your past. When you're pursuing God's promises without looking back, God will kill what's pursuing you.

> **Behavior Will Always Reveal the Real You**

The Israelites came to the wilderness. God was training them to change their behavior. He monitored their conversation and behavior. **What got them out of Egypt wasn't enough to take them into the Promised Land.**

No one wants to stay in the wilderness. No one wants to stay in slavery; but when you are living between two places, you have to be very careful that you don't forget how hard yesterday was. When it cost a lot to get into your future, it can be easy to look back.

This deceptive thinking will disqualify you for your next season. The children of Israel came out of slavery into welfare. In the wilderness, God did everything for them. He made sure their clothes, their shoes and their health never weaned. He led them with a cloud by day and with a fire by night. He went before them and behind them.

What got you here won't get you there. When they came to the end of the wilderness, God had to test their behavior to see if they believed that they belonged in promise. Behavior will always reveal the real you.

Prayer doesn't get you of the wilderness. Don't misunderstand me, prayer is important and necessary. Prayer may get you out of Egypt, but it will not take you into promise. Your behavior is the key to getting out of the wilderness. Do you believe that you belong?

Three things that will qualify you for your next season:

1. Your self-image.
2. Your conversation.
3. Your persuasion on where you belong.
   Do you believe you belong there? The proof is in your behavior. If you want to accelerate into your next season, start acting like you belong there.

3. **Crisis**: I can't write enough about crisis. Everyone will experience crisis. Crisis reveals you. Crisis, tribulation and delayed promises all force you to expose what you're really thinking. You are either in a crisis, coming out of a crisis or getting ready to enter a crisis. Crisis will inevitably happen. Monitor how you act in a crisis.

4. **Countenance:** Countenance is your posture, your facial expressions and your appearance. Haven't you ever looked at someone and knew immediately by their expressions exactly where they were in life?

"And the LORD said unto Cain, Why art thou wroth? and why is thy countenance fallen? If thou doest well, shalt thou not be accepted? and if thou doest not well, sin lieth at the door. And unto thee shall be his desire, and thou shalt rule over him." Genesis 4:6-7 KJV

*"Then the LORD said to Cain, "Why are you angry? Why is your **face downcast**? If you do what is right, will you not be accepted? But if you do not do what is right, **sin is crouching at your door**; it desires to have you, **but you must master it**." Genesis 4:6-7 NIV*

Cain's sin was tied to his countenance. Notice the text, *"face downcast."* Sin was waiting at the door to destroy Cain. God said something here that really moves me to think. He said, *"You must master it..."* One translation says, *"You must rule over him..."* Cain possessed the ability to master sin before the power of redemption, through his countenance, behavior and reactions.

This is powerful. Satan doesn't really know how situations and circumstances are affecting us unless we reveal it through our countenance. He can monitor facial expressions and posture and know immediately that what's going on around you is affecting what's going on within you. How many times have you given the enemy or a person the satisfaction of knowing what is happening to you is working by the look of your countenance? I know that I have done this many times.

5. **Reaction:** This is the sister to countenance. When your countenance has fallen your next movement is reaction. How you react can be costly in any situation. I have reacted wrongly in crisis so many times. I have since learned that my reactions can add longevity to my crisis. The children of God spent 40 years in the wilderness

simply because they had the wrong reaction to their crisis. The giants got their focus more than the promise. Your reaction is revealing you.

- What's your reaction to correction?
- What's your reaction to an instruction?
- What's your reaction to giving?
- What's your reaction to fear?

6. **Decisions:** Decisions reveal you. I was sitting in my office one day and the phone rang. It was Dr. Murdock. He said to me, *"Son, I have something to share with you that has changed my life."* This is what he said. *"Decisions decide wealth."* At first I thought, *"That's it? Three words, that's all you got?"* But after focusing on those three words I have come to this conclusion. Just about everything in our lives is attached to a decision. God gave me this about decisions. ***"Wrong decisions can trigger the law of unintended consequences."*** This explains why bad things happen to good people. It's not God's will or plan. Wrong decisions will create seasons that God never scheduled for us. Every decision creates consequence, good or bad.

You can stop hating God. You can stop hating your parents. You can stop blaming everyone for failure. *More than likely you are to blame. You made a wrong decision.* Decisions decide wealth. Here's something else Dr. Murdock said. *"Son, place any word in the place of wealth and you can change our life."* Replace wealth with joy, love, relationships, health and any word you can think of. Decisions decide joy... decisions decide relationships... decisions decide.... That's pretty powerful if you ask me.

7. **Pressure:** *Anything you are becoming is the result of pressure.* Pressure reveals you. The oil can't come out of the olive until it is pressed. Pressure reveals what you're really made of. How do you perform under

pressure? Some focus under pressure, others fold. Winners use pressure to create better focus.

How is a diamond made? It is made under years of extreme pressure. Out of the coal the diamond is formed. The coal sits in the soil of pressure. Most crumble and are absorbed into the soil of pressure, but every now and then a piece of coal doesn't fold, but uses the pressure to make something more valuable and harder than coal. Diamonds!

The anointed are more anoint*ed under pressure. That's when the oil is leaking every*where. Jesus became more anointed to save us because he was pressed on all sides. Pressed becomes processed. Never despise pressure. God is using it to make you. Storms are not meant to break you; they're meant to make you.

8. **Giving:** Giving is the biggest proof of your partnership. If you are unwilling to give to something, you have revealed your true opinion of it. Giving is the only proof of love. Love always wants to give. Love never takes. Love never looks to get. Giving is the proof of your focus.

Here's a powerful truth about giving. If you aren't happy with your present living, change your giving. Sowing seeds are the surest way to have a better tomorrow. God will never ask you to give what you don't have. He will always ask you to give something you want to keep. This is the test of commitment. God used this test more than once in the Bible. He used it with Abraham, He used it with Isaac, and He used it with the lad who had five loaves and two fish. Giving is so powerful for change that the enemy has distorted the minds of those in church to water down the principle of sowing seeds for financial harvest.

Religion uses the phrase, *"We aren't supposed to give to get."* Come on, how unreal and untruthful is this statement. No human on the earth was made or conditioned not to receive after they've done something. You confess Jesus as the Son of God and Lord of your life because you want to receive salvation. The whole salvation method is giving to get. You confess and give up your sins so that you can receive Jesus and His salvation for you.

Chapter Thirteen

RESTORATION
IS ATTACHED
TO TIMING

*"Life is all about **timing**... the unreachable become reachable, the unavailable become available, the unattainable... attainable. Have the patience, wait it out; it's all about **timing**." Stacey Charter*

*T*he only real gift God gave any of us is the gift of timing. Think for a moment. You didn't pick your mother or father. You had no say in where you would be born. No one asked you if you wanted to be a boy or a girl. You didn't decide the color of your hair, your eyes, nor did you have anything to do with your height. You had no power over what country you would be born in or what color of skin you would have.

The only real power we have is what we do with time. Time is your most precious commodity. The **designed life** will become a life that honors time.

When we experience loss, the first thing we must understand is that time also has been lost. Time is not our enemy; time is the vehicle that God uses to bring recovery. Let me encourage you; however long it takes for restoration to occur is a clue to how big your recovery will be. The harvest of loss is always increasing when God is the source of our restoration.

"Repentance is a gift." Loss is usually the consequence of wrong decisions, but repentance is the gift that we have to use God's grace as our recovery process. God has declared in His word that when the thief is discovered he has to return what he has stolen seven fold (Proverb 6:31). God uses time to our advantage. He gives us time to see our failures and allows us to judge ourselves before He sends judgment. I believe this is the power of grace. God is holding back judgment for a time and a season to allow us the opportunity to get our lives right through repentance. This is why it is very important that we don't judge others. God isn't judging them so why should we? We need to understand that restoration is the power of the Gospel. I can get back everything I've lost through God's love, by time and timing.

Time is our most powerful tool for gaining anything we desire or need on the earth.

WHAT TIME IS IT? It's time to get your money back!

Time is money! You have to spend your most precious gift of time for everything you want. Let's establish some guidelines for time. There is only a set amount of time given. For instance, there are only twenty-four hours in a day. That's all you get. There are only sixty seconds in a minute and sixty minutes in an hour. That's all you get. What you do with those minutes and hours will decide what you lose or gain in a day.

I like to call those time segments moments. There are many moments that make up a day. You really never have a bad day, just a bad moment within a day. Many people allow bad moments to ruin a whole day. This is nonsense. You need to arrest the moment that is bad so it does not illegally enter into the rest of your day and ruin it. Take control of the moments, so they do not take control of you. I've witnessed bad moments turn into months and years. Time is powerful!

Time is money! You spend the currency of time for anything you want in life. If a father wants to experience his children's activities, he will have to cash in the currency of his time. If you desire to know more, you will have to trade off time to study. If you need money, you sell your time to an employer and they pay you for your time.

Time is the key to a mastered life. Time is the key to wealth. Place time on your money and interest to your time and you have what some call compound interest. This powerful wealth key is that in time your money begins to attract more money. Wow! Time is a powerful master key! Think of all the people who don't save their money so that it will increase in time. Spending your money now robs you of your future increase in time. The old adage works here; ***Play now, pay later, or pay now, play later in time.*** Imagine how deadly it is to waste the only real commodity you have been given. That is time!

Three levels of time

1. Past
2. Present
3. Future

Many have allowed past time to infect and destroy present time. Your past is made up of your pain, your afflictions, your scars and your troubles. All of us have imprintings and regrets in our past. How we decide to let go of those wounds and allow them to heal will decide what you dream about in your present. This ultimately affects your future. This is all done by the power of time.

BATTLES ARE LOST AND WON BY TIMING

*"You win battles by knowing the enemy's **timing**, and using a **timing** which the enemy does not expect."* Miyamoto Musashi[ix]

I've heard of wars and battles lost just because of timing. Timing was essential for the battle fought in Normandy during World War II. It is said that if one moment would have changed we would have lost that great victory to Germany.

> **I Can Predict Your Success By Your Respect of Time!**

I read a story that illustrates what time is about. If you have 10 pounds of iron you can use it to earn money in three different ways. The time you decide to spend on this iron decides your income. The illustrations are as follows:

1) You can take your 10 pounds of iron, place it in fire, heat it up and beat it into horseshoes that would be worth about $30.00 worth of time.

2) You can use that same 10 pounds of iron and spend a little more time to make needles. This will be worth approximately $300.00 of time. Wow! Spending a little more time and effort can increase your financial income.

3) You can now take that same 10 pounds of iron, spend a little more time and make watch springs from it. Watch springs would be worth around $3000.00.

It's the same amount of iron used in three different ways, but adding time and effort to the equation will increase its financial worth.

Our time is much like this illustration. Think about how much time you have probably wasted. It makes me very upset to think how many things I would probably already know or have if I had spent my time better. I'm sure the same is true with you

God wants all of us to understand that time is the one thing on the earth that you cannot make more of and cannot be saved for a rainy day. Time is not prejudice; it doesn't stop for anyone.

If you don't decide what to do with your time, others will. Be very careful and laborious to evaluate all those who waste your time with trivial and meaningless conversation. Move swiftly away from time wasters. When you witness someone who is careless and flippant about their own time, know they will be flippant and careless with your time as well.

> **Champions Make Decisions That Create a Future They Desire. Losers Make Decisions That Create the Present They Desire.**

Time is a master key to your future. What you do today is deciding what you are becoming tomorrow. What are you doing today for a better tomorrow? If you're not satisfied with your present income, find another way to make more money. Invest time into it and see if you aren't happier in the future.

IT'S NOT JUST YOUR TIME, IT'S YOUR TURN

Most people have asked the question more than once, "God when will I see my harvest? Why hasn't it happened for me yet? Where am I going, and how am I going to get there?"

I was walking on the treadmill one day, listening to a song and thinking about my future, my anointing, and my talents. All of a sudden I found myself saying, *"It's my time. Lord, I know this is my season, this is my time."* Have you ever felt like it was your season or time? Within minutes of speaking out loud to the Lord I heard this voice within, say back to me, **"It's not just your time son, it's your turn."** I literally almost lost my footing as the spirit of the Lord came all over me.

First, we must understand what this really means; it's not just your time, it's your turn. Timing starts the process to your turn. David entered into his season of timing when Samuel anointed him to be king at Jesse's house. Timing is the moment when God begins to pull on you to be different. Timing is when God says you're ready for next. It was timing when Moses rose up and killed the Egyptian. It was timing when Daniel survived captivity and entered into the court of the enemy's kingdom.

Timing can create wonderful moments; however, it is not the finished work of your anointing. Timing can be a long season. Moses spent forty years in the wilderness before God appeared in the burning bush to call him off the bench, give him the opportunity to face Pharaoh and set His people free. Joshua walked eighty years in timing before God called him to face the

> **Faith That is Not Tested is a Faith That Cannot be Trusted.**

walls of Jericho. Timing may last a while, but when it's your turn it will only be a moment before the door of your next season is ready to open.

The door of next is decided by what you do and how you do it when it is your turn! Many get excited because they have been anointed in timing, never stopping to consider what's next after timing has found them. You will have to go through training and testing before it can be your turn!

A faith that is not tested is a faith that cannot be trusted. God usually does the unusual when He begins to set you up for your turn. You need to understand this to survive what's next. God's goal, plan and desires are not just about blessing you. God isn't working to give you a blessing or get you to the land of promise. God's dream and vision for your life is not to get you to the promise, but to keep you there. God doesn't want to give you a moment of blessing so you can pay a power bill, a house payment or even supply you with a onetime seed. His divine plan is to make you a lifetime blessing so that He can show off how good and powerful He is to others. His will is for you to be debt free so that you can be blessed to bless others. You should give God glory and Jesus praise for every miracle and blessing.

David didn't go straight into kingdom training camp after he was anointed by Samuel to be king. Timing was on him, but he wasn't ready for his turn. David went right back into the field to tend the herds for his father. If you are not faithful where you are at, you will never be faithful when you get to where you belong.

David had to fight a bear and a lion. He had to write worship songs and live alone in rejection. He waited for the moment that the door would open to call him off the bench of timing and into the arena to perform.

Performance is important when it is your turn.

You must be prepared and ready to show off what you have when your turn comes. So what have you been doing in your timing? I hope that you have been praying, killing bears, killing lions, and worshipping.

No one will care about your victories or open the door for your next season until you face your giant and kill it. You must perform well when it is your turn. Do you know how many people blow their moment of opportunity, their turn, simply because they didn't train, study or prepare in timing? Do not waste time, use this season you are in. Train your mind to think prosperous. Change how you talk, walk and move. Start acting like it's your turn. Don't worry; you will get another turn if you missed your last opportunity. God is a God of second and third chances, but the next time you are called off the bench, win! Show off! Perform and kill your giant so that the next season will materialize.

5 laws of the universe

1. Space
2. Time
3. Energy
4. Matter
5. Intelligent thought

Nothing on the earth, including you, would exist without these five ingredients. Space creates time, time creates energy and matter is produced out of energy. It takes intelligent thought to make the other four laws work together in harmony to build the world you see and experience.

Nothing you see on the earth just happened. If you study the laws of the earth and creation close enough, there is no way you can believe it all just happened by itself. Everything around you, including you, had a designer. God used words to create. God put intelligent thought into action and spoke into existence what we see. The same is true of us.

Genesis 1:1 says, *"In the beginning, God created..."* The earth was without form and void, and darkness was upon the face of the deep. The earth was in a chaotic state. Here's where this story gets interesting. God is always drawn to chaos. What good is being all-powerful if you can't show off what you possess? God entered chaos so He could exercise order over it.

The default of the earth is chaos. Entropy is the word I'm looking for. Entropy simply means that anything left alone on the earth will eventually turn to chaos or break down.

The only way to fix chaos is to put order into it. God's power was attracted to the earth when it was without form, dark and empty. God loves to enter chaos and call it to order. He's the force that is larger and bigger than chaos.

Order doesn't happen randomly

A lesser being cannot become a greater being without someone or something getting involved with its change. This is why it is so important to have a mentor who is in a higher place and position in life. Someone in a lower position than you cannot and will not increase you. If anything, they will pull you down to their level, especially if you're not in a position to mentor them and train them.

If the default of the earth is chaos, then we know that when there is chaos, someone has failed to exercise order!.

When God decided to do something about the void, formless, dark and chaotic world, He stood up and told it what He wanted it to become. God used words to create. He spoke to the situation and put order to chaos! Remember that order never happens randomly. When God spoke order into chaos, chaos formed itself into what God told it to be. I believe this same law is at work every single day. There will never be a day where we don't face situations, crises, problems and defeats (chaos). Instead of allowing the situation, the chaos, to completely destroy our faith and hope for a better life, we must stand up and face it with boldness. We must work the same law as God showed us in Genesis. We must speak to the chaos of our life and put order where there is disorder. What most of us do is complain about our pain; complain about our mountain. Many of us speak so much more about the situation, that we give the crisis power over us. We cry about it until we are so deep into the chaos that we have no revelation to speak God's word to it. Now we have lost all order. I want to encourage you to use your faith and command your situation to become what your revelation has decided it to be. Don't allow the crisis to define your day; allow your revelation to turn your situation around. Your problem is waiting for an instruction to move you into your next season.

NOTHING CAN CREATE EVERYTHING

What is space? Space is a dark open blanket of nothing. In God's world, 'nothing' never means nothing and 'zero' never means zero. Have I got your mind hurting? When God sees nothing, He is driven to create. With God *empty means opportunity*! *Less means more!* Out of space, out of nothing, God decided to create time. Time is the measurement of beginning and end. When time was established, laws were created. These laws of the universe are now for all to use and operate in. When we use these laws we can expect the same results as God. Out of nothing something was established. The end and beginning of all things came out of nothing. When time was fashioned and the clock began to tick, energy showed up. Energy was harnessed from God's word into God's laws that we call time, space and seasons (Hebrews 11:3).

Energy is the power that comes from someone working God's law to put order into chaos. When someone uses God's law of energy, they are using God's force. Energy brings power to force your situation to become what you have told it to be; with your faith you now are forming your world.

Energy creates matter. Matter is the substance of energy. When matter was established, things became possible. Trees, birds and all living things now have a doorway from which it can become. How did these four elements find their potential and become what they were always meant to be?

The potential came from *intelligent thought*. God appeared through the blanket of space and commanded light to be revealed. When God spoke, He was actually putting his thoughts into words. The four major elements came together and produced what they were told to be.

These four elements still exist today; *space, time, energy, and matter.* They are revealed in your life through want, nothingness, pain and crisis. If you would allow the Spirit of God within you to wake up, you can use your faith, open your mouth and command these four elements to be what you want them to be. I believe we call this being *"Born Again."* Crises, chaos, confusion and problems are the doors for your faith to show off what it can do. Believing will cause you to see it before it is manifested. It is alive and forming in your thoughts. Your words are putting your thoughts into power. They are making your thoughts to become a thing. So we know that THOUGHTS ARE THINGS!

Why do so many accept their life instead of try to change it? They have bought into a lie that what they have is all they can get. This has never been God's intent for us. He never created us to be enslaved to existing. God created us in His image and in His likeness. That means we need to look like Him with confidence and attitude. Likeness implicates that we have His same focus and power to live life to the fullest. We have the power to create order from chaos.

SUBDUE... *"Have Dominion..."*

God wasn't speaking just to be heard. This is the law! To subdue creates the power to have dominion. Subdue means to lean into chaos and pull order out of it. Get a mental picture of yourself leaning into the crisis, pain, or problem (chaos) and becoming stronger and tougher than the chaos. Grab it by the throat and force it to submit and become what you want it to be; not what it is trying to be. You have this power in you. It's called your faith. It's called your persuasion. When you understand this law, you will sit up in the midst of wherever you are and whatever you are going through and take charge.

Come on! Do it right now. Stand up and start declaring what you want your future to be. Stop accepting your life and start changing it right now. You are not created to earn a living; you are here to design your life.

Jesus says this law in **John 10:10, "... For I have come that you might have life and that you might have it more abundant."** I don't care what you've done. I don't care how old you are. It doesn't matter that your yesterday is full of wrong decisions and bad habits. The proof that God's mercy is still on you is that you are reading this book right now. That means you can change your life today. Yesterday is in the tomb, tomorrow is in the womb and what you do right now decides what you are going to birth. Let yesterday stay where it is, in the tomb. Stop resurrecting your failures, mistakes, guilt and shame. Do what they did when they placed Jesus in His tomb. Seal it and set guard over it. Lock up yesterday and never let it resurrect. Live for today and your future.

I believe that your tomorrow is looking brighter, right now!

CHAPTER FOURTEEN

CLIMATE DECIDES THE SEED'S MATURITY!

Good seed and good soil aren't enough!

*A*nother word for atmosphere is environment. Atmosphere is very important in your life. Many live life and never think about the atmosphere they wake up in, work in, hangout or even live in.

- Atmosphere decides how you feel.
- Atmosphere decides what you wear. *When you check the weather forecast you are actually checking to see what the atmosphere will be.*
- Atmosphere decides how you think, study and concentrate.
- Atmosphere creates faith or promotes doubt.
- Atmosphere defines winners.
- Atmosphere promotes peace or confusion.

ATMOSPHERE MATTERS

Years ago, I had a well know worldwide speaker at my church for the first time, Dr. Mike Murdock. This was a big event for me. First, we were just opening our new facility, and Dr. Murdock had agreed to fly in for three days to pray over and dedicate our new facility to the Lord. This was the most renowned speaker we had ever had. I was honored, humbled and nervous to have such a powerful man of God come minister to us. You can imagine how crazy things were and how nervous I was as we walked in the building. The service had already started. I walked behind Dr. Murdock carrying his brief case. He stopped abruptly and when he did, I ran right into his back. I felt so stupid! What happened next changed my life. Dr. Murdock looked up in the air, closed his eyes and just stood there. He then turned to me and said, *"Son always assess the atmosphere... atmosphere matters to God! Son, I like what I am sensing in this place."* My church and life have never been the same since that day.

You must labor to build the proper atmosphere; atmosphere will change your focus.

Always assess the environment

Assess the environment when you enter into a room where there is a group of people. Don't speak or say anything until you have discerned the atmosphere. You don't know what's already been discussed. The best way to enter an environment is with an open mind and a silent mouth.

I'll never forget when I entered a room shouting something funny, not even paying attention to who was in the room and what was going on. My entrance wasn't funny; it was actually an interruption to what was being discussed. I immediately felt the stares of those in the room and knew I had offended them. Why? Not because of what I said, but because I didn't assess the atmosphere. They were in a learning mood and I was trying to make it funny. My mentor looked at me and said, **"Son, always assess the environment!"**

Learning this master key will stop so many problems and arguments. Look at the life of Jesus. He always assessed the atmosphere. He would speak for hours when he was around people who were hungry for the information He possessed. He would stay silent when he assessed that those in the crowd didn't really care. I believe one of the reasons Jesus was successful in building a power network was that He operated in this law. He was always sensitive to the atmosphere.

BE AN ATMOSPHERE CHANGER

What is an atmosphere changer? An atmosphere changer is someone who turns the mood of a room into what they are feeling. They do this by their posture, sound and attitude.

I've witnessed someone enter a room and the spirit of faith be diminished immediately. They are atmosphere changers. This works in the positive as well as the negative. I've also witnessed someone enter the room and the spirit of doubt and confusion are lifted and a mood of faith enters.

Attitude creates atmosphere. It is important to remember that your attitude in any given situation creates atmosphere. Atmosphere decides what seeds God will plant in your life. Seeds decide harvests. So, if seeds decide your harvest, atmosphere decides what seeds will grow. If attitude creates atmosphere then you and I decide what harvests we are living with. If you don't like your harvest then change your seed. You must work on your attitude and atmosphere to do that.

I've heard all of my life that in order to have a harvest all you need is good soil and good seed. This is not entirely true. You can take pineapple seed and plant it in the rich soils of Midwest North America. It will grow. The seed will start its journey to fruition. It's not that there's not warm weather to start the growth in the Midwest, but the climate will change too soon. The cold weather will enter before the young plant can produce a harvest.

The truth is that you need good soil, good seed and the right climate for a seed to produce a harvest. Climate represents attitude. If the climate changes over your seed too soon then you will hinder its maturity. You'll see growth and experience the joy of watching the seed break through the soil, but that's all you will get. When the climate shifts the longevity of the seed, which is now a plant, can't finish its journey to harvest.

You and I have the power to plow the soil, sow the seed and keep the climate over that seed even when you're experiencing attack, delayment and harassment. Stay focused. Keep your praise and worship high! The climate over your seed matters greatly.

GOOD SEED AND SOIL ARE NOT ENOUGH!

I must also have the right climate. Climate represents atmosphere. I have no control over how the soil reacts. I have no control how the seed will react with the soil. I have no power to help the germination process. After I've sown, all I can do is wait.

I do have control over the climate. The climate is my responsibility. I must discern and learn about the climate. I must work it, watch it and make sure that my attitude doesn't shift over my seed. Attitude decides climate. I must guard and protect my attitude while I wait. I cannot allow people, crises and pain to shift my faith and begin to build wrong climate through my words and actions. This will stop my seed from its full maturity and me from receiving my harvest.

Make sure you guard your climate. Protect your environment. Don't allow anyone or anything to change your atmosphere of faith and expectation. Do not get into agreement with your crisis. Stay in agreement to your seed and your harvest.

My Thoughts on Prosperity

I've been on both sides of the fence in life. Those who believe in the message but live outside the parameters of Biblical prosperity have misrepresented the prosperity message.

I don't believe that God intended for us to exploit the prosperity message to a *giving or seed sowing 'only' message*.

There is more to this message than just emptying your savings to help others increase their empire. I do believe that sowing seed is a Kingdom principle and a natural law of multiplication. However, there has to be balance in all things.

God's purpose for man is to have life more abundantly. He placed man as the head in the order of creation. He gave us dominion! He gave us rule to subdue! He gave us the power of wealth and health. God's intent was for us to live life and not just to earn a living. God knows that we require money to work the power of exchange in this life. Unfortunately, when we speak about money, immediately the religious minds shut down and stop receiving.

Money will not bring you peace of mind or joy. I know people who have plenty of money, but their life is miserable. They have many family issues and lay awake at night with a restless mind. Money can buy you a house, but not a home! Money can buy you things, but not happiness. But money is needed. Money creates influence and power. I want you to have plenty of money! I desire that all God's children have financial freedom and are blessed to be a blessing.

The word "wealthy" incorporates all areas of life - money, family, relationships, peace, health and life.

Money without peace is not a wealthy life at all.

13 LAWS OF WEALTH

1. A Positive Mental Attitude
2. Physical Health
3. Harmony In Human Relationships
4. Freedom from Fear
5. The Hope of Future Achievements
6. The Capacity for Applied Faith
7. A Willingness to Share One's Blessings with Others
8. To Be Engaged in a Labor of Love
9. An Open Mind to all Subjects Towards all People
10. Complete Self Discipline
11. Wisdom With Which to Understand People
12. A Spiritual Freedom To Know You Are Okay With God
13. Financial Freedom

- *By: Napoleon Hill*

Notice that money is last on this list. This book is about life, health and wealth; a book that is going to help you start living the life God designed and paid for.

EVERYTHING NEEDS PROMOTION

Everything in your life needs promotion. I know it does in my life. I want everything to grow and become stronger; my love for God, my love for my wife, my love for life, my love for health. Everything in our lives needs to advance to its fullest potential.

Earning a living is stressful and painful. The God designed life is the life that wins! It is a life that is free to live, to laugh and to enjoy others. A God guided life is the life God intended for us to live.

"Delight yourself also in the Lord, and He shall give you the desires of your heart." Psalms 37:4 NKJV

Delight means to have fun. We have become so bogged down with debt and work that we have lost the true meaning of living. God never intended for us to live such a life of captivity. We have become bound to our own fears and false expectations. Many are living a life of sadness and depression simply because they don't know how to get out.

"Live a little." Live it up. God is not as starched as we have made him out to be. I'm not advocating a life of sin, but I am saying God wants us to be wealthy, healthy and above all, happy.

I have put together what I believe will help you achieve your dreams and your goals...master keys to unlocking the door that has been shut for too long.

Remember, your position in the Kingdom of God is recovery! When you understand your position, you can use these master keys to unlock the door to your tomorrow!

Decision Page:

May I Invite You to Make Jesus Christ the Lord of Your Life?

The Bible says, *"That if you will confess with your mouth the Lord Jesus, and will believe in your heart that God raised Him from the dead, you will be saved. For with the heart man believes unto righteousness; and with the mouth confession is made for salvation."* Romans 10:9,10

Pray this prayer with me today:
"Dear Jesus, I believe that You died for me and rose again on the third day. I confess to You that I am a sinner. I need Your love and forgiveness. Come into my life, forgive my sins and give me eternal life. I confess You now as my Lord. Thank You for my salvation! I walk in Your peace and joy from this day forward. Amen!"

Signed_____

Date_____

[Mail this in to Dr. Grillo]

☐ I made a decision to accept Christ as my personal Savior today, and I would like to be put on your mailing list.

Name_____

Address_____

City_____State _____Zip_____

Phone_____Email_____

FOGZONE MINISTRIES
P.O. Box 3707, Hickory N.C. 28603
828.325.4773 Fax: 828.325.4877 www.bishopgrillo.com

TO INVITE DR. JERRY GRILLO TO SPEAK AT YOUR NEXT CHURCH CONFERENCE, BUSINESS MEETING OR TO SCHEDULE TELEVISION OR RADIO INTERVIEWS,

WRITE TO:

FOGZONE MINISTRIES
ATTENTION: APRIL NARAIDU
P.O. BOX 3707 HICKORY, NC. 28603

OR EMAIL: FZM@FOGZONE.NET

FAX INVITATION TO 828-325-4877

OR CALL 1-888 FAVOR ME

Sources Used:

Master Key Eight: <u>Book Never Eat Alone</u>: By Keith Ferrazzi

<u>How Win Friends And Influence People</u>: By Dale Carnegie

Master Key Ten: Murdock, Dr. Mike. 19 Facts About Imagination: Wisdom Commentary Volume 2.

All Definitions were retrieved from a web source.

[i] Source Unknown. Chinese Proverb
[ii] Web Source. http://www.buzzardhut.net/index/htm/Babylon/Nimrod.htm. 2012
[iii] Web Source. http://www.buzzardhut.net/index/htm/Babylon/Nimrod.htm. 2012
[iv] Source Unknown
[v] Web Source. http://www.oppapers.com/essays/Attitude-Organisation-Behaviour/285179. 2012
[vi] Web Source. http://www.yourdictionary.com/attitude. 2012
[vii] Hill, Napoleon. Think and Grow Rich: The 21st Century Edition: Revised and Updated. High Roads Media. 2004
[viii] Web Source. http://www.yourdictionary.com/imagination. 2012
[ix] Web Source.http://thinkexist.com/quotation/you_win_battles_by_knowing_the_enemy -s_timing-and/216502.html.2012

Made in the USA
Lexington, KY
23 November 2013